The
Scrumptious
Veggie
Cookbook

For Kids
and Others

CM0079872O

The
Scrumptious
Veggie
Cookbook

For Kids
and Others

Marianne Bird

Cartoons by Mark Glanford

GREEN
PRINT

First published in 1991 by
Green Print
an imprint of The Merlin Press
10 Malden Road, London NW5 3HR

© Marianne Bird

The right of Marianne Bird to be identified as author of this work has been asserted in
accordance with the Copyright, Design and Patents Act 1988.

All rights reserved. No part of this publication may be reproduced, stored in a
retrieval system, or transmitted, in any form or by any means electronic, mechanical,
photocopying, recording or otherwise, without the prior permission in writing of the
publisher.

ISBN 1 85425 058 2

1 2 3 4 5 6 7 8 9 10 :: 99 98 97 96 95 94 93 92 91

Phototypeset by Computerset, Harmondsworth, Middlesex

Printed in England by Biddles Ltd., Guildford, Surrey on recycled paper

Contents

This book is dedicated to Mrs Wise, my
cookery teacher at Chipping Campden
School, who taught me many useful skills.
I am also grateful to my mother for advice with
some of the recipes and my father for helping
me write the book.

Introduction

This cookery book is meant for children between six and sixteen who like the idea of making delicious meals and snacks but want to use 'green' recipes which do not include meat or fish. It has been specially written to meet an ever-growing need, as more and more young people turn away from eating meat and change to a vegetarian or near-vegetarian diet.

Until only a few years ago there were not many vegetarians at schools, but now they number many thousands and school meal organisers are having to take this more and more into account. Many boys and girls are rightly appalled at the widespread maltreatment of animals and do not like the idea of animals suffering so that they can eat meat. They are also alarmed at what they learn from the press, radio and television about such terrible illnesses as Mad Cow Disease, another strong argument why meat-eating should be avoided or gradually reduced.

The recipes given in this book are therefore intended to satisfy the demand for all kinds of tasty and attractive meatless meals, snacks and delicacies. Vegetarian meals need never be dull, indeed far from it, they can be absolutely delicious. Recipes for tasty snacks and special treats to celebrate Christmas and Easter are given, as well as for such events as Pancake Day, Bonfire Night, Mother's Day, Father's Day and, of course, St. Valentine's Day! A little effort in preparation and care when mixing the ingredients and cooking them will bring results that will gladden the hearts (and stomachs!) of everyone.

Many of the meals and snacks described in this book are cheaper to make and easier to prepare than those involving the use of meat. A sign of the times is that many food shops and supermarkets now offer a wide range of vegetarian foods and ingredients.

Young cooks aged between six and twelve may need help from a parent or older brother or sister when preparing and cooking food.

To all the boys and girls who like this book and use the recipes in it I wish great success and much happy eating!

Marianne Bird

Safety in the kitchen

ALWAYS USE KNIVES CAREFULLY

Cooking is fun, but before you begin there are some important things to remember.

Hygiene
Always make sure that your hands are clean before you begin.
Make sure that utensils and work surfaces are clean.
Protect your clothes when you cook – wipe-clean aprons are ideal.
Remember to wash up when you have finished and leave the kitchen clean and tidy.

Safety

Always have an adult or an older brother or sister on hand to help you, especially when lighting gas cookers.

Always use knives carefully.

Turn handles on pans inwards so they do not get knocked over.

Always use oven gloves when you handle hot pans or dishes, especially when taking things from the oven.

If you have to use an eye-level grill and you cannot reach it, do not stand on a chair. Get help from an adult.

Never touch anything electrical with wet hands – you could get a shock. If you must handle electrical appliances make sure that your hands are thoroughly dry.

Before you begin

Read through the recipe carefully so that you know exactly
what you are going to do.

Make sure you have all the ingredients you need.

Always prepare the cake tin before you start making the
cake mixture. Grease the inside of the tin well and line it with
greased greaseproof paper or baking parchment.

Always pre-heat the oven. It needs time to reach the correct
temperature – allow 15 minutes before you want to use it.

All quantities are for four people unless otherwise
mentioned.

Sugar
Most of the cake and pastry recipes given in this book contain
only moderate amounts of sugar. However, a few have a
somewhat larger sugar content and it is important to
remember that all these delicious and scrumptious foods
which contain sugar are intended as 'treats' for special
occasions and certainly not for regular eating! Too much sugar
is bad for your teeth as well as adding to your weight, so it is
best to avoid using it too much or eating high sugar-content
foods regularly.

Try always to use raw cane sugar rather than white sugar. If
necessary this can be powdered in a grinder.

Other ingredients
Where margarine is mentioned in the recipes vegetarian
margarine is meant.

Use wholemeal flour and not white flour whenever possible.

Measurements

Measure ingredients carefully and accurately, using kitchen scales and measuring jugs.

All spoon measures are level spoonfuls unless otherwise stated.

Presentation

Make the finished dishes look as appetising as you can. Add garnishes for colour.

If you are serving a hot dish, remember to warm plates or dishes beforehand. Put them in a cool oven for a few minutes.

Tips for young cooks

Pastry is less likely to shrink during cooking if it is allowed to rest in a cool place or refrigerator for 10-15 minutes before rolling out and again just before baking. Cover it with greaseproof paper.

Use egg whites at room temperature to obtain the best results during beating.

When beating or whisking, put a damp cloth under the bowl as this will stop it moving on the surface.

You can cook pancakes in an ungreased frying pan if a little vegetable oil is added to the batter.

Faults in cake making and the causes

If a cake sinks in the middle, it is often the result of not using enough flour or using too much raising agent in proportion to the amount of flour. Another cause can be opening the door of the oven before the cake has set or moving the cake while it is still rising.

A dry cake may be caused by overbaking, which removes too much moisture. Dryness of the cake can also be caused by using too much raising agent.

Fruit sinking to the bottom of the cake may be due to the use of too much fruit in proportion to the other ingredients. If the cake mixture is too wet the fruit will also sink as the liquid evaporates.

Uneven rising of the cake may be caused by baking at too high a temperature, which causes the cake to set around the sides while the centre is still rising. Placing the cake too close to one side of the oven also will result in uneven rising. Always put the cake tin in the centre of the oven shelf.

To prevent a cake sticking to the tin after baking, the tin should be greased and floured or lined with greaseproof paper before the mixture is put in.

How to cook perfect pasta

Half-fill a large saucepan with boiling water. You will need 2 to 3 litres/4 to 6 pints of water to 450g/1lb of dry pasta or 225g/8oz of fresh pasta. Add a pinch of salt and a tablespoon of oil, to avoid the water boiling over, then stir the pasta into the pan, gradually coiling it in, while making sure the water is kept on the boil. Dried pasta generally takes from 7 to 15 minutes if cooked steadily and fresh pasta will take from 2 to 4 minutes.

Stir the pasta occasionally while it is cooking to avoid sticking. To find out if the pasta is cooked, take a little from the pan, allow it to cool a little and then try it. It should taste cooked and also keep its shape. Finally, drain the pasta in a colander and stir in a tablespoon of olive oil or a knob of margarine to prevent it sticking together.

Baking parchment

I could not manage without baking parchment, a special kind of parchment suitable for all baking needs which will stand temperatures of up to 230°C/450°F or gas mark 8. You do not need to grease baking tins when you use this parchment, but you can do this sometimes if the food should be given a lighter texture.

Baking parchment is also a boon to cooks because when making biscuits, for example, it gives a beautiful finish on the base.

Words used in cookery and their meaning

Beat Mix briskly with a wooden spoon, turning the mixture over and over with a circular motion to mix in the maximum amount of air.

Blend Mix until smooth. When using a liquidiser or food processor to blend, all ingredients must be cool, or the steam could blow the lid off.

Chill Put food in the fridge to cool, without freezing.

Consistency The firmness or thickness of a mixture. Soft dropping consistency for instance is used for a mixture that when lifted up on a spoon will gently drop back when the spoon is turned upside down.

Core Take out the seedcase and pips of fruit such as apples.

Cream Mix fat and sugar briskly with a wooden spoon until light and fluffy and pale in colour.

Crush Generally used for garlic. Peel the garlic clove, then push it through a garlic press or chop it finely.

Dice Chop or cut into small rectangular pieces.

Fold in Incorporating ingredients into a whisked or creamed mixture by putting the, usually dry, ingredients on top and with a metal spoon lightly scooping the creamed mixture over them, so trapping air in between. This is repeated till all ingredients are thoroughly mixed.

Frying In shallow frying a small amount of fat is used in a shallow pan and the food has to be turned halfway through the cooking time to cook both sides. In deep frying a large deep pan is used in which the food is totally immersed in hot oil.

Knead Lightly working dough with your hands until it is smooth, using a circular movement and bringing the outside into the centre every time.

Pinch A measure (usually of salt) – as much as you can pick up between forefinger and thumb.

Roll out Using a rolling pin, flatten a ball of dough on a floured surface till a sheet of the thickness you require is formed. Always roll in one direction only.

Rub in Combine fat and flour by cutting the fat into small pieces with a knife and then, using your fingertips, rubbing it into the flour till the mixture resembles breadcrumbs. Keep everything, including your hands, as cool as possible.

Separate (eggs) Crack the egg shell carefully over a bowl to form two halves. By pouring the egg from one half shell into the other the white will gradually drop into the bowl, while the yolk remains in the shell. Be very careful when doing this so as not to break the yolk on the sharp edges of the shell.

Shred Slice finely using a knife or grater, or tear into small pieces.

Sieve Put ingredients such as flour through a sieve to get rid of lumps and add air.

Whisk Add air and stiffen ingredients such as egg whites by beating very rapidly using a fork or a hand or electric whisk.

Salads

Minty fruit salad

125ml / 4fl.oz unsweetened apple juice
1 red eating apple, cored and sliced
1 green eating apple, cored and sliced
2 ripe pears, sliced
3 satsumas, peeled and segmented
2 bananas, peeled and sliced
1 tablespoon chopped fresh mint
fresh mint spray to decorate

1. Put the apple juice in a bowl and add the fruit and chopped mint.
2. Toss gently till all fruit is coated in apple juice. Cover and chill until ready to serve. Decorate with a spray of fresh mint.

Waldorf salad

4 sticks of celery
50g / 2oz walnuts
1 large dessert apple
175g / 6oz Cheddar cheese
150mls / ¼ pint mayonnaise
salt and pepper to taste

1. Chop the celery and walnuts.
2. Wash the apple, dry and cut into quarters. Remove the core from each quarter and dice the apple.

3. Cut the cheese into cubes.
4. Mix all the ingredients in a bowl.

Potato salad

450g / 1lb new potatoes
1 small onion
salt and pepper
1 teaspoon finely chopped parsley
1 tablespoon mayonnaise
vegetable or sunflower oil

1. Scrape the potatoes, cook them, drain and dice while still hot.
2. Chop the onion finely and lightly fry in a teaspoon of vegetable or sunflower oil.
3. Add a dessertspoonful of onion, the parsley and mayonnaise, and salt and pepper to taste to the diced potato and mix thoroughly but lightly with a fork.

This is delicious when served cold!

Green salad

1 lettuce
bunch of watercress
4 dandelion leaves
small amount of mustard and cress
pinch of salt
pepper
1 tablespoon vinegar
2 tablespoons salad oil

1. Wash the lettuce leaves in slightly salted water (do not oversalt!), and also the bunch of watercress, the dandelion leaves and a little mustard and cress. Drain thoroughly.
2. Shred the lettuce and dandelion leaves, add the mustard and cress, and mix in the watercress and a pinch of salt. Dust lightly with pepper.
3. Mix the vinegar and oil thoroughly and use as a dressing.

Pasta salad

275g / 10oz broccoli
175g / 6oz wholemeal pasta spirals
1 tablespoon olive oil
salt and pepper
2 tablespoons chopped nuts

1. Half-fill a large saucepan with lightly-salted water. Bring to the boil and add the pasta. Bring back to the boil and cook until tender, 7 to 15 minutes.
2. Cook the broccoli for about 9 minutes in boiling water. Drain.
3. Mix the pasta and broccoli. Stir in the oil and nuts. Add salt and pepper to taste.

Can be eaten hot or cold.

Chicago dip

175g / 6oz peanuts, shelled
25g / 1oz margarine
4 tablespoons natural yoghurt
2 dessertspoons chopped raisins
celery, cucumber, carrots, apple

1. Put the peanuts in a blender with the margarine and purée until very smooth.
2. Pour into a bowl and stir in the yoghurt and chopped raisins. If the mixture is too thick add a little skimmed milk.
3. Serve with celery sticks, fingers of cucumber, carrots, wedges of apple.

Tomato salad

3 large tomatoes
$^1/_2$ large cucumber
110g / 4oz white Cheshire cheese
4 tablespoons French dressing
lettuce leaves

1. Chop the tomatoes and dice the cucumber and cheese.
2. Mix with the French dressing in a bowl and toss well.
3. Serve on a bed of lettuce leaves.

Lunches, snacks, suppers

Skyscraper sandwich (for one)

3 slices brown bread
margarine to spread
cucumber slices
1 tomato, sliced
lettuce leaves, washed and dried
1 tablespoon mayonnaise
$\frac{1}{2}$ small onion, peeled and sliced
two large mushrooms, peeled and sliced
salt and pepper to taste
watercress to garnish

1. Spread the slices of bread with margarine on one side.

2. Chop the lettuce and and put it into a bowl. Add the cucumber, tomato, onion, mushrooms and mayonnaise, with salt and pepper to taste and mix.

3. Spoon half the salad onto one slice of bread, put the next slice of bread on top. Place the remaining salad on top of this slice.

4. Place the third slice of bread, spread side down, on top and very carefully cut the sandwich in half with a sharp knife. Put on a plate garnished with watercress and serve.

SKYSCRAPER SANDWICH

Ben's burgers

Ben is a 'green' dairy farmer from Cornwall who loves all animals. His cooking is a joy to eat!

Cooking time: 6 minutes

110g / 4oz oats
2 large eggs
175g / 6oz Cheddar cheese, grated
1 large carrot, grated
1 tablespoon sesame seeds
1 tablespoon tomato purée
$\frac{1}{2}$ teaspoon Cayenne pepper
2 teaspoons mixed herbs
breadcrumbs for coating

1. Mix the oats with the cheese, eggs, carrot, sesame seeds, tomato purée, Cayenne pepper and mixed herbs. Make sure that you do this thoroughly.

2. Shape the mixture into 8 round burgers and coat these with breadcrumbs.

3. Lightly fry the burgers for about 3 minutes on each side.

4. Serve with a crisp green salad or coleslaw.

Pitta bread pizza (for one)

Cooking time: a few minutes

1 large wholemeal pitta bread split in half
1 tablespoon tomato purée
50g / 2oz Double Gloucester (or any other) cheese, grated
2 tomatoes, sliced
2-3 spring onions, finely chopped
few slices of red or green pepper
sprinkle of mixed herbs
1 pineapple ring, chopped
salt and pepper to taste

1. Spread the tomato purée over the pitta bread, put on the rest of the ingredients.

2. Place the pitta bread under the grill and cook for a few minutes until the cheese starts to bubble and turns a lovely golden colour.

3. Serve on a warm plate with a salad or just on its own.

No cooking appetizer

275ml / ¹⁄₂ pint Greek yoghurt
1 garlic clove, peeled and crushed
¹⁄₂ teaspoon salt
¹⁄₄ teaspoon ground cumin
1 spring onion, trimmed and chopped

1. Pour the Greek yoghurt into a large jug, add the crushed garlic, and stir thoroughly.

2. Add the cinnamon and cumin and again stir well.

3. Place the jug in the fridge and chill for about an hour.

4. Pour into a serving dish and sprinkle with the chopped spring onion.

5. Serve with tortilla chips or with vegetable dishes.

Crunchy mini quiches

Cooking time: 15 minutes

50g / 2oz margarine
2 eggs
175g / 6oz wheat flakes
1 tablespoon flour
150ml / ¹⁄₄ pint natural yoghurt
75g / 3oz Double Gloucester cheese, grated
1 leek, washed, trimmed and finely chopped
salt and pepper to taste
chopped chives or mixed herbs

1. Crush the wheat flakes.

2. Melt the margarine in a saucepan, add the crushed wheat flakes and mix well.

3. Divide the mixture between six 7½cm / 3in quiche tins and use your fingers to evenly cover the base and sides of the tins with the crumb mixture.

4. Put the eggs into a bowl with the sieved flour and the yoghurt and whisk it all together. Then add the chopped leek and stir with a wooden spoon until this is mixed in. Add salt and pepper to taste and stir again.

5. Divide the egg mixture between the 6 tins, and sprinkle some grated cheese on top. Scatter a few chopped chives or some mixed herbs over the cheese, to give added flavour.

6. Place the tins on a baking tray and cook in a pre-heated oven at 190°C / 375°F or gas mark 5 for 15 minutes until the egg mixture is firm and golden-coloured.

7. Take the mini quiches out of the oven and allow them to cool for about 40 minutes. Then carefully loosen the edges of the flans so that you can remove them from the tins. Serve them with hot crusty rolls or an attractive salad, or on their own.

Field fare

A delicious starter or accompaniment to a main meal.

Cooking time: 18-20 minutes

110g / 4oz fresh wholemeal breadcrumbs
1 tablespoon corn oil
1 tablespoon fresh parsley
1 tablespoon fresh thyme
1 garlic clove, skinned and crushed
4 large mushrooms, without stalks
50g / 2oz Gouda cheese, grated

1. Gently heat the oil in a frying pan and fry the breadcrumbs and garlic for 4 minutes or until the breadcrumbs become slightly crispy.

2. Take the frying pan off the stove, add the parsley and thyme and stir.

3. Place the mushrooms with their hollow sides upwards in an ovenproof dish and fill with the breadcrumb mixture. Sprinkle with grated cheese.

4. Put into the oven and bake at 190°C / 375°F or gas mark 5 for 18-20 minutes. Serve with a salad and crusty brown rolls.

Egg nut balls

Cooking time: 35 minutes

675g / 1^1/$_2$lb potatoes
1 tablespoon fresh parsley
40g / 1^1/$_2$oz Cheddar cheese, grated
4 hardboiled eggs
ground salt and pepper
1 tablespoon plain flour
90g / 3^1/$_2$oz peanuts, chopped
1 egg white, beaten
10g / ^{1}/$_2$oz margarine

1. Peel and cook the potatoes. Drain, mash with the margarine and pepper and salt to taste. Add the grated cheese and the fresh parsley. Leave to cool.

2. Lightly roll the shelled hardboiled eggs in the flour. Flour your hands and divide the potato mixture into 4 portions. Wrap each egg in the potato mixture so the egg is completely covered. Now dip them into the beaten egg white, then roll in the chopped peanuts.

3. Place the egg balls on a greased baking tray. Cook for 35 minutes until crispy and golden at 200°C / 400°F or gas mark 6. Serve hot or cold, they are delicious with salad.

Cheese pudding

Cooking time: 45 minutes

1 small onion
110g / 4oz wholemeal breadcrumbs
110g / 4oz Cheddar cheese, grated
2 eggs
1 teaspoon French mustard
450ml / ¾ pint chilled milk
¼ teaspoon pepper
¼ teaspoon salt
parsley to garnish

1. Peel and roughly chop the onion.

2. Put all the ingredients apart from the parsley in a liquidiser and blend until smooth.

3. Pour the mixture into a greased shallow ovenproof dish and bake in the oven at 200°C / 400°F or gas mark 6 for about 45 minutes, until set and golden brown.

4. Sprinkle with chopped parsley and serve hot from the dish.

Savoury bread and butter pudding

Cooking time: 35-40 minutes

8 large slices of wholemeal bread
margarine to spread
225g / 8oz grated cheese (any kind)

1 onion, grated
4 eggs, beaten
575ml / 1 pint fresh milk
salt and pepper to taste
pinch of dry mustard

1. Spread the bread lightly and cut into small cubes.
2. Grease an ovenproof dish, spread half the bread cubes in the bottom of the dish, cover with half the cheese, then the onion. Add the rest of the bread and top with the remaining cheese.
3. Mix the beaten eggs with the milk and salt and pepper, and pour this mixture over the pudding.
4. Bake in a moderate oven, 180°C / 350°F or gas mark 4, for about 35-40 minutes until set and golden. Serve hot.

This is nice with salad on a summer's day or with cooked vegetables in the winter.

Rigby's pies

Cooking time: 25 minutes

16 thin slices of brown bread
50g / 2oz melted margarine
225g / 8oz tin of unsweetened baked beans in tomato sauce
50g / 2oz Cheddar cheese, grated
paprika for garnishing

1. Using a large pastry cutter cut 8 circles from half the bread slices, just enough to cover the base and sides of 8 10cm / 4in patty tins. Brush both sides of the bread circles with some melted margarine.

2. Line the patty tins with the bread circles, pressing down well. Divide the baked beans between the tins.

3. Cut 8 circles just big enough to cover the pies from the rest of the bread, and brush both sides with the remaining margarine. Put on top of the pies, pressing firmly around the edges to seal.

4. Sprinkle the cheese over the top and bake at 200°C / 400°F or gas mark 6 for 25 minutes, until golden brown and crisp.

5. Remove from the tins and sprinkle with paprika. Serve hot.

Tasty lunchtime bite

Cooking time: 30-35 minutes

110g / 4oz margarine, melted
175g / 6oz wholewheat crackers
75g / 3oz Cheddar cheese, grated
3 eggs, lightly beaten
150ml / $\frac{1}{4}$ pint milk
$\frac{1}{2}$ cucumber, cut into thin slices
1 small carton natural yoghurt
pinch of salt and pepper
1 tablespoon chopped fresh chives

1. Crush the crackers and mix thoroughly with the margarine, then press this mixture over the base and sides of a 20cm / 8in flan dish.

2. Spread the cucumber slices on the prepared base.

3. Put the yoghurt, eggs, milk and grated cheese in a bowl and stir well. Pour this mixture over the cucumber. Sprinkle with salt and pepper and the chopped chives.

4. Place the flan dish on a baking tray and cook in the oven at 180°C / 350°F or gas mark 4 for about 30-35 minutes until the filling is set and a lovely golden-brown in colour.

5. Serve with rice or sweet potatoes or on its own.

Winter warmer soup

Cooking time: 20 minutes

25g / loz margarine
350g / 12oz mushrooms, sliced
25g / loz ground hazelnuts
425ml / $^3/_4$ pint vegetable stock (use a stock cube)
425ml / $^3/_4$ pint milk
$^1/_4$ teaspoon grated nutmeg
pinch of salt
freshly-ground black pepper
3 tablespoons single cream

1. Melt the margarine in a large pan, add the mushrooms and stir over a medium heat for 2-3 minutes until the juice runs. Put the lid on the pan and simmer gently for 5 minutes.
2. Stir in the ground hazelnuts, add the vegetable stock, milk, nutmeg, salt and pepper to taste. Cover the pan and simmer gently for 10 minutes.
3. Blend the soup in a liquidiser until smooth.
4. Return the soup to the rinsed-out pan and heat gently, stirring all the time, until hot but not boiling.
5. Serve immediately with crusty brown rolls.

Makes a very appetising soup.

Easy omelette (for one)

If possible do try to use a special omelette pan with a thick base so that when it is heated the omelette will cook quickly. Over-cooking or slow cooking produces a tough texture.

10g / $^1/_2$oz margarine
3 large eggs
pepper and salt

1. Whisk the eggs lightly to mix the yolks and whites thoroughly together. Add salt and pepper to taste.
2. Melt the fat over a brisk heat, tilting the pan so as to allow the sides to become greased as well.
3. Pour the eggs into the pan, tilting it backwards and forwards. Allow to set on the underside, brown it slightly if you like but make sure the top does not set. Turn the omelette onto a warm plate and serve at once.

Cheese and nut balls

110g / 4oz cream cheese
110g / 4oz peanuts
salad cream to moisten
salt and pepper to taste

1. Mix the cream cheese with some salad cream and season to taste with salt and pepper. Form the mixture into little balls.
2. Grind the nuts coarsely in a blender.
3. Roll the balls in the nuts. Serve with an attractive salad.

Any day vegetable dish

Cooking time: 10-12 minutes

450g / 1lb courgettes, cleaned and sliced
225g / 8oz mushrooms, peeled and sliced
25g / 1oz margarine
1 clove garlic, peeled and crushed
2 tablespoons vegetable oil
1 teaspoon freshly chopped parsley
pinch of salt and pepper

1. Melt the margarine in a large frying pan, add the crushed garlic and vegetable oil and stir.
2. Add the sliced vegetables and parsley, stirring regularly, so that everything is evenly cooked, till just tender. This will take about 10-12 minutes.
3. Season to taste and put in a warmed serving dish. Must be served hot!

Vegetable crumble

Cooking time: 60-65 minutes

1 medium onion, peeled and chopped
3 tablespoons tomato purée
$\frac{1}{2}$ teaspoon tabasco sauce
1 tablespoon vegetable oil
2 garlic cloves, peeled and crushed
250g / 9oz broccoli, separated into florets and sliced pieces of stalk
225g / 8oz tin tomatoes, roughly chopped

crumble topping:
25g / 1oz melted margarine
25g / 1oz porridge oats
2 tablespoons sunflower seeds
2oz wheatgerm

1. Pour the oil into a large pan and heat it. Add the garlic, onion and broccoli stalks, cover and simmer over a gentle heat for about 12 minutes, stirring now and then.
2. Then add the tabasco sauce, tomato purée, chopped tomatoes and broccoli florets, stirring thoroughly with a wooden spoon. Put the lid back on the saucepan and cook for another 10-12 minutes over a gentle heat.

3. Prepare the topping for the crumble by putting all the ingredients in a bowl and mixing.
4. Carefully put the vegetables into an ovenproof dish and cover with the crumble topping. Place in the oven and cook at 190°C / 375°F or gas mark 5 for 35-40 minutes until a lovely golden colour.
5. Serve hot with jacket potatoes or with an attractive fresh salad.

Scrambled eggs with tomato

Cooking time: 5 minutes

6 eggs, beaten
150ml / ¼ pint semi-skimmed milk
10g / ½oz margarine
2 tomatoes, roughly chopped
dash of Worcester sauce, to taste
wholemeal toast, to serve

1. Beat the eggs and milk together. Melt the margarine in a heavy-based saucepan over low heat. Add the eggs and cook, stirring all the time, until the eggs begin to set.
2. Add the tomatoes and Worcester sauce and continue cooking until set but still moist. Serve at once with toast.

Corny lunch

Cooking time: 50-60 minutes

2 large eggs
110g / 4oz plain flour
1 teaspoon sea salt
½ teaspoon black pepper

575ml / 1 pint milk
375g / 13oz fresh or frozen sweetcorn kernels

1. Sift the flour into a basin, add the salt and pepper.
2. Crack the eggs into a separate bowl, whisk them lightly with a fork. Add to the sifted flour and stir in thoroughly. Pour in the milk gradually, beating all the time. Then add the sweetcorn.
3. Grease an ovenproof dish and pour in the batter, place in the oven and cook at 180°C / 350°F or gas mark 4 for 30 minutes. When cooked it should look golden-brown. Serve hot.

Savoury slices

I was given this recipe by an aunt who, whenever I stayed with her, used to make them for me.

Cooking time: 35-40 minutes

175g / 6oz Cheddar cheese, grated
150g / 5oz porridge oats
1 egg, beaten
50g / 2oz margarine
pinch of salt and pepper
$^{1}/_{2}$ teaspoon rosemary

1. Put all the ingredients in a bowl and mix well.
2. Spoon the mixture into a small shallow cake tin, make sure you press it down in the tin.
3. Bake in the oven at 180°C / 350°F or gas mark 4 for 35-40 minutes, until golden.
4. When cooled a little cut into slices and allow to go cold before eating.

Tresillian bread

Cooking time: 35-40 minutes

110g / 4oz cornmeal
110g / 4oz self-raising flour
2¹/₂ tablespoons baking powder
75g / 3oz curd cheese
350ml / 12fl.oz semi-skimmed milk
¹/₂ tablespoon salt
110g / 4oz carrots, scrubbed and finely grated

1. Lightly grease and line the bottom of a shallow 18cm / 7in square baking tin.
2. Sieve together the cornmeal, flour and baking powder, add the bran left in the sieve.
3. Blend the cheese, milk and salt together in a separate bowl.
4. Stir the carrot into the flour, then gradually stir in the milk mixture.
5. Pour into the prepared tin and bake at 190°C / 375°F or gas mark 5 for 35-40 minutes or until pale golden in colour.
6. Turn out of the tin and serve hot or cold.

Debbie's quick dish

Cooking time: 10 minutes

350g / 12oz pasta shells
110g / 4oz walnut halves
225g / 8oz ricotta cheese
2 tablespoons chopped fresh herbs
3 tablespoons lemon juice
2 tablespoons olive oil
pinch of salt and pepper
grated cheese to serve

1. Place the pasta in boiling water and cook for 10 minutes or until tender.

2. Meanwhile finely chop the walnuts in a blender, then add the cheese, herbs, lemon juice and oil and purée until smooth.

3. When the pasta is cooked, drain and season, and spoon into warm bowls. Pour the walnut sauce over the pasta, sprinkle cheese on top and serve immediately.

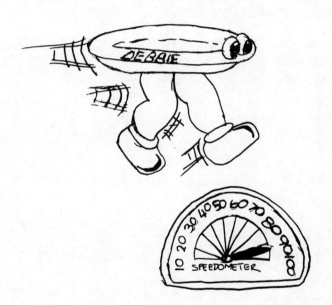

Express paté

This paté is lovely when served with hot wholemeal rolls or pitta bread.

450g / 1lb low-fat soft cheese
2 tablespoons fresh mixed herbs or 1 tablespoon dried herbs
2 garlic cloves, skinned and crushed
50g / 2oz walnuts, chopped
chopped fresh herbs and walnuts to garnish

1. Put all the ingredients apart from the garnish into a blender and mix well.
2. Spoon into a dish, smooth the top, cover and chill for 10-15 minutes.
3. Serve garnished with herbs and walnuts.

Robert's cheese snack (for one)

Cooking time: a few minutes

75g / 3oz Cheddar cheese, grated
25g / 1oz chopped nuts
2 slices of bread, lightly toasted
pepper to taste
milk to mix

1. Put the grated cheese, nuts and salt and pepper in a bowl and mix. Add some milk to give a smooth, creamy consistency.
2. Spread the mixture on the lightly toasted bread and cook under a hot grill until brown and bubbly.
3. Transfer to a warm plate and serve with a salad or baked beans.

Picnic treats

Cooking time: 10-12 minutes

Makes: 18-20

450g / 1lb self-raising flour
$1/2$ teaspoon salt
1 teaspoon mustard powder
110g / 4oz margarine
225g / $1/2$lb Lancashire cheese, grated
4 tablespoons fresh chives, chopped small
275ml / $1/2$ pint milk

1. Put the flour, salt and mustard powder into a bowl, rub in the margarine until the mixture resembles fine breadcrumbs.
2. Stir in the cheese and chives, add the milk and mix to a soft dough, then knead quickly until smooth.
3. Roll out to just over 1cm / $1/2$in thick on a floured surface, cut into rounds with a 5cm / 2in cutter, and brush the tops with some extra milk.
4. Transfer to baking trays and cook for 10-12 minutes until golden at 230°C / 450°F or gas mark 8.

These are nice hot or cold, with butter or a slice of cheese. If you cannot get fresh chives, use spring onions instead.

Herb balls

Makes: 12-14

450g / 1lb mashed potatoes
2 egg yolks
2 heaped tablespoons flour
3 tablespoons wholemeal breadcrumbs

vegetable oil
herbs of your choice
salt to taste

1. Mix the mashed potatoes with most of the egg yolk and the flour. Add some salt and a good quantity of herbs. Form into small balls.
2. Dip each ball into the remaining egg yolk and roll in the breadcrumbs.
3. Deep-fry in vegetable oil until golden-brown. Serve hot.

Cheese straws

Cooking time: 5-8 minutes

50g / 2oz Parmesan cheese
50g / 2oz plain flour
50g / 2oz margarine
pinch of cayenne pepper

1. Sieve the flour into a bowl and rub in the margarine till the mixture resembles fine breadcrumbs.
2. Add a pinch of cayenne pepper and the cheese and stir in a little water to bind the dough together.
3. Roll out thinly on a floured board, cut into thin straws, transfer to a baking tray and bake for 5-8 minutes in the oven at 180°C / 350°F or gas mark 4.

Hummus

This is a Mediterranean favourite of mine. You can serve it as a starter or a snack, with a salad or pitta bread.

425g / 15oz tin of chick-peas, drained and rinsed
5 tablespoons olive oil
2 garlic cloves, skinned
1 small slice of wholemeal bread without crust
grated rind and juice of ½ lemon
pinch of salt and pepper
2 tablespoons tahini or 1 egg, beaten

1. Put all the ingredients in a blender and mix until smooth.
2. Put into a bowl, cover and chill for 2½-3 hours.

Cheese and onion dip

110g / 4oz margarine
110g / 4oz cream cheese
2 finely chopped spring onions or 2 teaspoons chopped
chives
1 teaspoon paprika
chopped onion or chives to garnish

1. Cream together the margarine and cream cheese, beat in
the spring onions or chives and add the paprika.
2. Spoon the mixture into a small serving bowl and decorate
with chopped chives or onions.

Serve as a dip with cheese biscuits. This also makes a
delicious topping for baked potatoes.

Potato wedges

Cooking time: 25-30 minutes

450g / 1lb potatoes, scrubbed
25g / 1oz margarine
salt and pepper to taste
110g / 4oz self-raising flour

1. Boil the potatoes for about 20 minutes until they are soft.
Drain thoroughly and leave to cool, then peel them.
2. Mash the potatoes well with the margarine, add seasoning
and beat in the flour to form a soft dough.
3. On a lightly-floured surface, roll the dough out into an
18cm / 7in circle. Place on a lightly-greased baking sheet and
cut into 8 wedges.
4. Bake at 220°C / 425°F or gas mark 7 for 25-30 minutes, until
risen and a crisp golden brown.

Delicious when served hot with herb butter or vegemite.

Herb and garlic bread

Cooking time: 20 minutes

1 wholemeal or granary stick
2-3 garlic cloves, skinned and crushed
3 tablespoons chopped fresh herbs such as chives, fennel,
dill, basil or parsley
50g / 2oz margarine
pepper to taste

1. Cut the loaf in half lengthways.
2. Blend together the garlic, herbs, margarine and pepper,
then spread the mixture on the bread.

3. Put the halves back together, wrap tightly in aluminium foil, shiny side inward, and cook in the oven for 20 minutes at 200°C / 400°F or gas mark 6.
4. Serve sliced, while still piping hot.

Spiced fingers

Cooking time: 2-3 minutes

6 slices of bread
margarine for spreading
4 dessertspoons caster sugar
2 dessertspoons ground cinnamon

1. Mix the sugar and cinnamon in a bowl.
2. Toast the bread slices on both sides, then spread on one side only.
3. Sprinkle the mixed cinnamon and sugar over the toast. Put under the grill for 2-3 minutes, cut into fingers and serve.

Winter evening snack (for one)

Cooking time: 1-2 minutes

2 slices of wholewheat toast
margarine to spread
1 teaspoon ground cinnamon
1 tablespoon honey

1. Spread the toast with margarine and place the slices on the grill tray. Spread the honey over the slices of toast, then sprinkle with cinnamon.
2. Place the grill tray under the grill and cook for a few minutes until the honey begins to bubble.
3. Serve at once on a warm plate.

McNab's porridge

This is a delicious variation of traditional porridge.

Cooking time: 5-7 minutes

10g / $^{1}/_{2}$oz bran flakes
175g / 6oz medium oatmeal
275ml / $^{1}/_{2}$ pint milk
275ml / $^{1}/_{2}$ pint water
2 tablespoons clear honey, to serve

1. Mix the bran flakes, oatmeal, milk and water in a saucepan and bring to the boil, stirring continuously.
2. Lower the heat and let the porridge simmer gently for 5-7 minutes, stirring occasionally, until smooth and creamy.
3. Pour into 4 warmed bowls, top each with $^{1}/_{2}$ tablespoon of honey.

Benjamin's pasties

Many people have their own version of pasties. This is mine.

Cooking time: 30-35 minutes

pastry:
450g / 1lb self-raising flour
110g / 4oz margarine
110g / 4oz white vegetable fat
pinch of salt
4 tablespoons cold water

filling:
4 vegetable burgers, crumbled
225g / 8oz raw mixed vegetables: onion, potato, carrot, turnip
175g / 6oz Cheddar or Double Gloucester cheese, grated
1 teaspoon sage
$\frac{1}{2}$ teaspoon salt
a little freshly ground black pepper
1 beaten egg for glazing

1. Sieve the flour and salt into a bowl and rub in the fats with your fingertips till the mixture resembles fine breadcrumbs. Sprinkle the cold water over the mixture and stir in with the blade of a knife till it forms a stiff dough. If necessary knead lightly.
2. Peel and dice the vegetables and put them in a mixing bowl. Add the crumbled burgers, sage, grated cheese, salt and freshly ground black pepper. Mix with a wooden spoon.
3. Roll out the pastry thinly on a lightly floured surface and cut out rounds using a saucer or small cake tin.
4. Brush the edges of the pastry lightly with water and spoon some of the filling into the centre of each pastry circle. Bring up the sides so that the edges meet in the middle, press them well together and flute with your fingertips. Brush the top of the pasties lightly with beaten egg.

5. Place them on a baking tray and bake in the oven at 220°C / 425°F or gas mark 7 for 10 minutes, then reduce the heat to 180°C / 350°F or gas mark 4 and cook for a further 20-25 minutes until a lovely golden colour.

6. Take the pasties out of the oven and serve hot, or leave on a wire rack to cool and serve cold.

These can be frozen if desired.

Main dishes

Nutcracker roast

Cooking time: 50-60 minutes

40g / 1½oz margarine
1 medium onion, chopped
1 stick of celery, chopped
225g / 8oz mixed nuts (walnuts, hazelnuts and peanuts in equal
quantities), coarsely chopped
3 large tomatoes, chopped
175g / 6oz fresh wholemeal breadcrumbs
pinch of salt
freshly ground black pepper
1 teaspoon mixed dried herbs
¼ teaspoon chilli powder
2 eggs, lightly beaten
watercress to garnish

1. Grease a small loaf tin and line it with greaseproof paper.
2. Melt the margarine in a large pan, add the onion and
celery and fry gently for about 5 minutes without browning.
3. Add the tomatoes, breadcrumbs, nuts, salt and pepper to
taste, mixed herbs and chilli and stir well. Next, add the
beaten egg and mix to a fairly soft consistency.

4. Spoon the mixture into the prepared loaf tin, cover with oiled baking foil. Place in the oven at 220°C / 425°F or gas mark 7 for 50-60 minutes.
5. When cooked, ease off the foil and run a knife around the sides of the tin. Turn the nutcracker roast onto a warm dish, garnish with watercress and serve.

Tomatoes in the hole

Cooking time: 30 minutes

6 large tomatoes
1 tablespoon melted margarine
1 tablespoon chopped parsley or chives
575ml / 1 pint milk
3 eggs, beaten
225g / 8oz flour
25g / 1oz breadcrumbs
seasoning to taste

1. Sieve the flour and seasoning to taste into a bowl. Stir in the beaten eggs mixed with half the milk, beat well, gradually adding the rest of the milk, until the batter is smooth.
2. Put the tomatoes into a bowl of boiling water for 1 minute, then remove and peel off the skins. Cut off the tops and take out the centres. Be very careful as peeled tomatoes are often slippery.
3. Mix the melted margarine with the breadcrumbs and the herbs and some seasoning. Fill the tomatoes with this mixture.
4. Put the tomatoes in a greased ovenproof dish and pour the batter over them. Bake in the oven at 220°C / 425°F or gas mark 7 for about 30 minutes.

Claudia's lasagne

Cooking time: 40-45 minutes

175g / 6oz pre-cooked lasagne
2 tablespoons olive oil
450g / 1lb onions, peeled and sliced
4 large mushrooms, peeled and sliced
425g / 15oz tin of chopped tomatoes
110g / 4oz grated cheese
freshly ground black pepper
pinch of salt

cheese sauce:
25g / 1oz flour
25g / 1oz margarine
275ml / ½ pint skimmed milk
50g / 2oz Cheddar cheese, grated
1 teaspoon mustard powder
pinch of salt and pepper

1. Fry the onions and mushrooms in the olive oil until they become tender, then remove the pan from the heat and allow to cool a little.
2. Now make the cheese sauce. Put the margarine in a saucepan and melt over a gentle heat. Stir in the flour, cook for a few seconds until the flour begins to bubble around the edges. Pour in about one third of the milk. Stir thoroughly until the sauce becomes very thick and smooth. Add the rest of the milk, again stir very well, and bring to the boil while stirring all the time. A smooth, medium-thick sauce should now be the result. Remove the saucepan from the stove and stir in the grated cheese, mustard powder and salt and pepper.

3. Place a layer of one third of the lasagne in the bottom of a greased shallow ovenproof dish. Put half the onions, mushrooms and tomatoes on top and season with salt and freshly ground pepper, sprinkle on one third of the grated cheese.

4. Repeat these layers and finish with the remaining lasagne. Spread the cheese sauce over the top so that the lasagne is completely covered.

5. Sprinkle with the remaining grated cheese and bake in the oven for 40-45 minutes at 200°C / 400°F or gas mark 6.

Hartwell pie

Cooking time: 30 minutes

1 onion, chopped
3 small carrots, scrubbed and chopped
1 tablespoon olive oil
1 green pepper, cored, seeded and chopped
400g / 14oz tin of tomatoes
2 tablespoons plain flour
150ml / ¼ pint vegetable stock
110g / 4oz mushrooms, chopped
salt and pepper to taste
½ teaspoon dried mixed herbs
675g / 1½lb potatoes, peeled and cut into small pieces
2 tablespoons semi-skimmed milk
2 tablespoons chopped fresh parsley
425g / 15oz tin of red kidney beans, rinsed and well drained
400g / 14oz tin of cannellini beans, rinsed and well drained

1. Heat the oil in a saucepan, add the onion, carrots and green pepper and cook gently for 10 minutes or until soft. Stir in the flour and cook for 2 minutes more.

2. Add the tomatoes and their juice, stock, mushrooms, dried herbs and seasoning to taste. Cover and simmer for 15 minutes, then remove the lid and cook for a further 15 minutes, stirring occasionally.

3. Meanwhile, put the potatoes into a saucepan with a small amount of boiling water. Cover and simmer for 10-15 minutes until tender. Drain and mash, adding the milk and parsley.

4. Add the kidney and cannellini beans to the tomato mixture and spoon into a shallow ovenproof dish. Pipe or spoon the mashed potatoes over the tomato bean mixture.

5. Bake in the oven at 200°C / 400°F or gas mark 6 for 30 minutes. Serve hot.

Peanut burgers

Cooking time: 10 minutes

2 medium-size onions
2 tablespoons vegetable oil
225g / ½lb peanuts, chopped
50g / 2oz wholemeal breadcrumbs
1 tablespoon chopped parsley
sea salt and freshly ground black pepper
25g / 1oz margarine
2 eggs
1 tablespoon tomato purée – optional

1. Chop the onions and fry gently in the oil without browning.

2. Combine the nuts and the breadcrumbs in a mixing bowl and stir in the parsley, salt and pepper. Add the cooked onion and rub in the margarine.

3. Mix in the eggs, to bind the ingredients. Add some tomato purée if you like.

4. Shape the mixture into 4 burgers and grill them, turning once, until they are brown on both sides.

Lasagne Milano

Cooking time: 35 minutes

Serves: 5-6

12 sheets pre-cooked lasagne
2 tablespoons vegetable oil
1 garlic clove, crushed
1 large onion, finely chopped
2 celery stalks, finely chopped
2 carrots, finely chopped
110g / 4oz button mushrooms, sliced
400g / 14oz tin chopped tomatoes
175g / 6oz lentils
pinch of salt and ground black pepper
25g / 1oz wholemeal breadcrumbs
25g / 1oz Cheddar cheese, grated

sauce:
50g / 2oz margarine
50g / 2oz plain flour
425ml / ¾ pint milk
110g / 4oz Cheddar cheese, grated

1. Heat the oil in a frying pan. Add the garlic and onion and cook for 2 minutes, add the carrots and celery and cook for a further 5 minutes, stirring all the time.
2. Stir in the mushrooms, tomatoes, lentils and seasoning and simmer gently for 15 minutes until everything is soft.
3. In the meantime make the sauce. Melt the margarine in a saucepan and stir in the flour, let it cook for 1 minute. Remove from the heat and stir in the milk gradually, be careful the mixture has no lumps. Return to the heat and bring to the boil, stirring all the time until the sauce thickens. Remove from the heat and stir in the grated cheese and seasoning.

4. Cover the bottom of a large ovenproof dish with 4 sheets of lasagne. Spoon half the filling on top, cover with 4 more sheets of lasagne and the rest of the filling and finally the remaining lasagne.

5. Pour the cheese sauce over the top and sprinkle with cheese and breadcrumbs.

6. Cook in the oven at 180°C / 350°F or gas mark 4 for 35 minutes until golden brown.

7. Serve hot with fresh crusty wholemeal or wholewheat rolls or with a fresh salad.

Butter bean bake

Cooking time: 30 minutes

3 courgettes, thickly sliced
3 leeks, trimmed and thickly sliced
25g / loz margarine
25g / loz plain flour
425ml / ³/₄ pint milk
pinch of salt and pepper
2 400g / 15oz tins of butter beans, drained and rinsed
6 tablespoons chopped fresh parsley
25g / loz fresh wholemeal breadcrumbs
50g / 2oz Cheddar cheese, finely grated

1. Cook the leeks and courgettes in a small amount of water until just tender, about 5 minutes, then drain.

2. Melt the margarine in a saucepan, add the flour and cook for 1 minute. Take off the heat and gradually add the milk, make sure there are no lumps. Bring to the boil, stirring all the time, until the sauce thickens. Season to taste.

3. Add the leeks, courgettes, butter beans and 4 tablespoons of parsley to the sauce and mix well.

4. Pour the mixture into an ovenproof dish, sprinkle with the breadcrumbs, cheese and remaining parsley.
5. Cook in the oven at 200°C / 400°F or gas mark 6 for 30 minutes.

This is delicious served with a crisp salad or with brown wholemeal rolls.

Fulbrook bake

Cooking time: 15 minutes

675g / 1¹/₂lb potatoes
125g / 4¹/₂oz margarine
3 tablespoons milk

salt and ground pepper
pinch of nutmeg
175g / 6oz oats
$1/2$ teaspoon mustard powder
175g / 6oz grated cheese

1. Peel and cook the potatoes. Drain and mash with 70g / $2^1/2$ oz of the margarine, milk, salt and pepper to taste and nutmeg. Put in a greased ovenproof dish.
2. Melt the remaining margarine and mix in the oats, mustard powder and cheese. Spread this mixture on top of the potatoes.
3. Bake in the oven at 190°C / 375°F or gas mark 5 for 15 minutes.

Delicious served with vegetarian bangers or salads.

Veggie stroganoff

Cooking time: 10 minutes

2 onions, sliced
1 garlic clove, skinned and crushed
2 tablespoons corn oil
225g / 8oz mushrooms, sliced
350g / 12oz tomatoes, sliced into wedges
400g / 14oz tin of chick-peas, drained
salt and pepper to taste
275ml / 10fl.oz low-fat natural yoghurt
1 tablespoon chopped gherkin
1 tablespoon chopped fresh parsley

1. Heat the oil in a large frying pan or saucepan, add the onion and cook for 3 minutes. Add the garlic and mushrooms and cook for 2 minutes more, then add the chick-peas and tomato wedges and cook for a further 3 minutes, stirring frequently, until the chick-peas become lightly browned and the tomatoes are softened.

2. Stir in the yoghurt and chopped gherkin and season. Heat gently, stirring, but make sure it does not boil otherwise the yoghurt will curdle.

3. Turn into a serving dish, sprinkle with the chopped parsley and serve at once with rice or baked potatoes and a salad.

Cheddar bake

Cooking time: 50 minutes

575ml / 1 pint milk
1 medium-size onion, finely chopped
4 eggs
225g / 8oz Cheddar cheese, grated
pinch of salt and pepper
175g / 6oz wholemeal breadcrumbs

1. Beat the eggs with the salt and pepper. Stir in the grated cheese, chopped onion and wholemeal breadcrumbs.

2. Pour this mixture into an ovenproof dish. Place in the oven and cook at 190°C / 375°F or gas mark 5 for about 50 minutes, until well-risen and golden-brown.

3. Serve hot with cooked vegetables, rice or potatoes or with a crisp salad.

Cheese and potato dish

Cooking time: 1 hour

2 thick slices of wholemeal bread
1 cup of milk
1 large onion
4 large potatoes, peeled
2 large eggs, beaten
50g / 2oz margarine, melted
50g / 2oz cheese, grated
1/2 level teaspoon marjoram
pinch of garlic salt
seasoning to taste
pepper, tomato and parsley to garnish

1. Soak the bread in the milk. Meanwhile, grate the raw potatoes and onions into a mixing bowl. Mash the bread and add to the mixture, together with the margarine, marjoram and garlic salt, eggs and most of the cheese. If you wish, add salt and pepper, but bear in mind that cheese itself is salty.
2. Grease an ovenproof dish thoroughly and pour in the mixture, topping it with the rest of the cheese.
3. Bake for 1 hour at 180°C / 350°F or gas mark 4. To make this dish even more enticing decorate before serving with slivers of red or green peppers, tomato slices and parsley.

Derek's burgers

Cooking time: 10 minutes

1 medium-sized onion, chopped
110g / 4oz of grated carrot
350g / 12oz tofu
2 teaspoons mustard seeds

1 tablespoon olive oil
1 teaspoon dried mixed herbs
2 teaspoons ground coriander
2 teaspoons cumin
2 tablespoons dark soy sauce
110g / 4oz wholemeal breadcrumbs
pinch of salt and pepper
4 baps

1. Heat the oil in a frying pan and gently cook the onion and carrot for 2-4 minutes.
2. Add the mustard seeds and stir until everything becomes soft. Leave to cool.
3. Mash the tofu into a paste in a bowl, then add the breadcrumbs, cumin, coriander, mixed herbs and soy sauce, mixing thoroughly.
4. Now add the onion, carrots and mustard seeds and stir well. Add salt and pepper to taste.
5. Shape the mixture into 4 burgers and cook under a pre-heated grill for about 10 minutes, turning them once.
6. Serve in baps, with a salad if you wish.

The Old Vicarage special

Cooking time: 6-8 minutes

2 eggs, beaten
25g / 1oz breadcrumbs
1 medium-sized onion, chopped
1 tablespoon soy sauce
1 teaspoon oregano
450g / 1lb tofu
$^{1}/_{2}$ teaspoon basil
vegetable oil for frying

sauce:

1 tablespoon vegetable oil
1 large onion, finely chopped
2 teaspoons fresh lemon juice
4 tablespoons malt vinegar
2 tablespoons cold water
5 tablespoons brown sugar
400g / 14oz tin of chopped tomatoes
pinch of salt and pepper

1. Crumble the tofu into a large bowl, add the rest of the ingredients and mix well, using a wooden spoon.
2. Shape the mixture into small balls.
3. Make the sauce. Heat the oil and gently fry the onions till soft. Add the tomatoes, stir, and then all the other ingredients. Stir very well, lower the heat and simmer for about 4 minutes.
4. Heat a little vegetable oil in a frying pan and gently fry the tofu balls till they are golden, 6-8 minutes.
5. Serve the tofu balls on a bed of rice, pour the sauce over the top.

Pasta sauce 'herby'

This is a lovely sauce which can be served with any kind of pasta. For the best way to cook pasta see p. 7.

75g / 3oz Parmesan cheese, finely grated
25g / 1oz ground almonds
2 garlic cloves, peeled and crushed
200ml / 7fl.oz olive oil
75g / 3oz chopped fresh herbs of your choice: chives, mint, parsley, dill, basil etc.

1. Mix the chopped herbs with the Parmesan cheese. Then add the crushed garlic and ground almonds and stir well.

2. Gradually pour in the olive oil, stirring all the time. It is important to make sure that everything is mixed thoroughly.

3. Pour the 'Herby' sauce over the cooked pasta and serve.

Puddings and desserts, hot and cold

Summertime queen

Cooking time: 20 minutes

4 slices brown bread without crusts
2 heaped tablespoons walnuts
425ml / ¾ pint milk
2 eggs, separated
grated rind of 1 lemon
75g / 3oz light brown sugar
225g / 8oz raspberries
fresh cream to serve

1. Cut the bread into cubes and put in a deep greased ovenproof dish. Sprinkle on the nuts.
2. Heat the milk in a saucepan until slightly warm.
3. Put the egg yolks and lemon rind into a bowl. Remove the milk from the heat and beat well into the egg mixture. Stir in 1 tablespoon of sugar. Pour this mixture over the bread and bake in the oven for 20 minutes at 180°C / 350°F or gas mark 4.
4. Carefully mix most of the raspberries with 1 tablespoon of sugar and spread them over the cooked custard.
5. Whisk the egg whites until very stiff, whisk in the remaining sugar, then swirl over the raspberries. Return to the oven for 10-15 minutes until the meringue is crisp.
6. Decorate with raspberries and serve with fresh cream.

Mother's pudding

Cooking time: 30 minutes

175g / 6oz caster sugar
50g / 2oz margarine
4 eggs, separated
575ml / 1 pint milk
juice and grated rind of 2 lemons
50g / 2oz plain flour

1. Cream the margarine with the sugar.
2. Mix the egg yolks with the milk and the lemon juice and rind. Beat well into the margarine and sugar, then fold in the sieved flour.
3. Whisk the egg whites until stiff, fold them into the other ingredients.
4. Spoon into a greased soufflé dish and place it in a roasting tin half filled with water. Bake for 30-35 minutes at 180°C / 350°F or gas mark 4.
5. Leave to cool before serving.

Fowey delights

This recipe was passed down from my great-grandmother.

Cooking time: 4-6 minutes

50g / 2oz plain flour
pinch of salt
2 teaspoons salad oil
4 tablespoons lukewarm water
1 egg white
8 thin slices of wholemeal or wholewheat bread without crusts
margarine for spreading
strawberry jam or plum jam

oil for frying
caster sugar
cinnamon

1. Sieve the flour and salt into a basin, make a well in the centre and add the oil and half of the lukewarm water. Beat the mixture till smooth, then gradually beat in the rest of the water.
2. Make 4 sandwiches with the bread, margarine and jam and cut them into squares or triangles.
3. Whisk the egg whites till they are stiff, then fold them into the batter.
4. Dip the sandwiches into the batter and fry in hot oil in a deep-frying pan until they are golden brown.
5. Drain on crumpled kitchen paper, then sprinkle with caster sugar and cinnamon and serve.

Ice palace

Cooking time: 1-2 minutes

1 Swiss roll filled with jam, cut into 4 slices
4 scoops vanilla ice cream

meringue:
3 egg whites
175g / 6oz caster sugar

1. Whisk the egg whites in a bowl until they are stiff and dry and stand in firm peaks. Add the caster sugar a little at a time, whisking thoroughly between each addition until the mixture becomes very thick and glossy.
2. Put the slices of Swiss roll on a baking sheet and top each with a scoop of ice cream.
3. Spoon the meringue mixture over the ice cream and Swiss roll, making sure they are completely covered.

4. Bake near the top of the oven at 240°C / 475°F or gas mark 9 for 1-2 minutes until the meringue takes on a golden tinge. Serve at once.

Devon dumpling

Cooking time: 40-45 minutes

450g / 1lb cooking apples, peeled, cored and sliced
50g / 2oz sultanas
25g / 1oz light muscovado sugar
2 tablespoons ground cinnamon

topping:
50g / 2oz plain wholemeal flour
50g / 2oz plain flour
50g / 2oz margarine
110g / 4oz porridge oats
3 tablespoons clear honey

1. Mix the apples, sultanas, sugar and cinnamon in a bowl, and spoon into an ovenproof dish.
2. In another bowl, mix the flours and rub in the fat until the mixture looks like fine breadcrumbs. Then stir in the oats and honey.
3. Sprinkle the topping over the apples and bake at 180°C / 350°F or gas mark 4 for 40-45 minutes until golden.
4. Serve with ice cream or custard.

Antonio's venetian delight

Cooking time: 40-45 minutes

110g / 4oz macaroni
575ml / 1 pint milk
1 large cooking apple, peeled, cored and chopped
50g / 2¹/₂oz raisins
grated rind of 1 lemon
1 tablespoon brown sugar
1 egg, separated

topping:
1 large apple, peeled, cored and sliced
25g / 1oz margarine, melted

1. Put the macaroni and milk in a saucepan, bring to the boil, cover and simmer for 12 minutes. Remove from the heat.
2. Add the chopped apple, raisins, lemon rind and sugar. Beat in the egg yolk.
3. Whisk the egg white until stiff and fold into the other ingredients.
4. Carefully spoon the mixture into a greased ovenproof dish and bake for about 30 minutes at 180°C / 350°F or gas mark 4.
5. Arrange the apple slices over the top of the pudding and brush with the melted margarine. Return to the oven and bake until the apple slices are golden, about 10 minutes. Serve with ice cream.

Caraway cobbler

Cooking time: 1 hour

275g / 10oz flour
40g / 1¹/₂oz caraway seeds
175g / 6oz caster sugar

2 eggs, beaten
110g / 4oz margarine
1 teaspoon baking powder
3-4 tablespoons water
pinch of salt

1. Sieve the flour, salt and baking powder into a bowl, then rub in the margarine until the mixture resembles fine breadcrumbs. Add the caraway seeds, sugar and beaten eggs, mix well. Add the water and mix to a smooth consistency.

2. Put the mixture into a small greased loaf tin. Bake for about 1 hour at 190°C / 375°F or gas mark 5 until golden.

Can be served sliced on its own or with margarine or jam.

Dive-in fondue

Dessert fondues are great fun to eat! You will need a heavy-
based pan or special fondue pan standing on a tripod over a
spirit burner or candle. Use long-handled forks to dip
whatever you fancy into the fondue – cubes of sponge cake,
marshmallows, pieces of fresh fruit, etc.

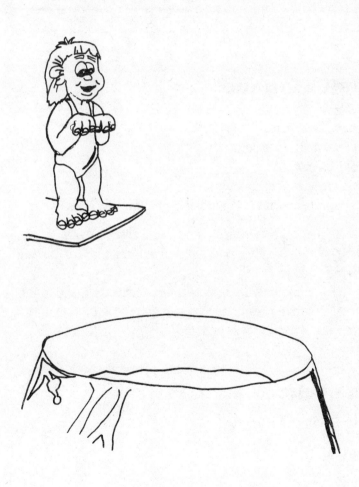

350g / 12oz marshmallows
6 tablespoons cream or milk
a few drops lemon juice
50g / 2oz almonds, finely chopped

1. Put the marshmallows and cream or milk in a fondue pan over a low heat and stir till the marshmallows have melted.
2. Then add the lemon juice and chopped almonds and stir till hot but not boiling.
3. Serve at once.

Devil's fondue

50g / 2oz margarine
175g / 6oz molasses sugar
350ml / 12fl.oz milk
2 tablespoons black treacle
2 tablespoons cornflour blended with 4 tablespoons water

1. Gently heat the margarine and sugar in a saucepan until the sugar dissolves. Bring to the boil and simmer for 1 minute while stirring.
2. Add the milk, treacle and blended cornflour. Bring to the boil again, stirring continuously, and simmer for 2-3 minutes.
3. Pour into a fondue pan and serve.

Barbecued bananas

Cooking time: 15 minutes

4 bananas, peeled
110g / 4oz almonds
50g / 2oz Barbados sugar
150ml / ¼ pint double cream

1. Place the peeled bananas in the centre of a double piece of cooking foil and sprinkle on the nuts and sugar. Fold the foil over the bananas to make a parcel.
2. Bake for 15 minutes on a cool part of the barbecue.
3. When cooked, spoon into 4 bowls and top with dollops of cream.

Pineapple upside-down pudding

Cooking time: 30 minutes

50g / 2oz margarine
50g / 2oz caster sugar
50g / 2oz self-raising flour
1 egg
small tin of pineapple rings
7 glacé cherries
caster sugar
custard or cream to serve

1. Cream the margarine and sugar until light and fluffy. Beat in the egg, then fold in the flour.
2. Grease an 18cm / 7in sandwich tin and sprinkle with caster sugar.
3. Make a pattern in the bottom with pineapple and cherries, and spread the cake mixture over this.
4. Bake in the oven at 180°C / 350°F or gas mark 4 for about 30 minutes.
5. Turn out onto a serving dish and serve upside-down, either with custard or with fresh cream.

Barbados dream

Cooking time: 2-4 minutes

6 bananas
275ml / ½ pint whipping cream
2 tablespoons dark Barbados sugar

1. Chop the bananas roughly.
2. Whip the cream till stiff and mix with the banana.
3. Spoon into a shallow ovenproof dish and sprinkle with
Barbados sugar. Put under the grill for a minute or two until
the sugar has melted.

Apple snowballs

Cooking time: 30-40 minutes

4 large cooking apples
2 heaped tablespoons brown sugar
4 cloves
1 teaspoon cinnamon
1½ dessertspoons caster sugar
3 egg whites
fresh cream to serve

1. Peel and core the apples and place on a greased baking
tray in the oven at 180°C / 350°F or gas mark 4 for 15 to 25
minutes until soft. Remove from the oven and put the apples
into a large ovenproof dish.
2. Mix the brown sugar and cinnamon and fill the centre of
each apple with this mixture and a clove.
3. Whisk the egg whites and caster sugar until stiff. Cover
each apple with whisked egg white.
4. Bake in the oven at 170°C / 325°F or gas mark 3 for about 15
minutes or until the meringue is set.
5. Serve hot with fresh cream.

Poor knights of Windsor

This is a traditional recipe that has remained very popular and is easy to make.

Cooking time: 4-6 minutes

8 slices of bread without crusts
margarine for spreading
6 tablespoons strawberry jam
1 egg, beaten
275ml / ½ pint milk
50g / 2oz margarine
1 tablespoon oil
1 tablespoon caster sugar

1. Spread the slices of bread with margarine and sandwich them together with the jam. Cut into thick fingers.
2. Beat the egg and milk together in a bowl and dip the bread fingers into this mixture using a large spoon.
3. Heat the margarine and oil in a frying pan, adding a little more during cooking if it is needed.
4. Fry the bread fingers on both sides until golden.
5. Drain on crumpled kitchen paper and dust with caster sugar. Serve.

Apple treat

Cooking time: 30-40 minutes

4 thick slices of one-day old bread
margarine to spread
4 dessert apples
110g / 4oz granulated sugar
25g / 1oz margarine

1. Spread the bread with margarine and put in a greased ovenproof dish, spread sides up.
2. Peel and slice the apples and arrange half the slices on the bread. Sprinkle with granulated sugar. Put a second layer of apple slices on top and sprinkle with the remaining sugar.
3. Cut the margarine into small cubes and dot over the top.
4. Cook in the oven at 180°C / 350°F or gas mark 4 for 30-40 minutes till golden-brown.

Delicious served with ice-cream or fresh cream.

Nancy's cheesecake

Nancy is a West Country farmer's wife who takes in stray cats and dogs and who has always been like a favourite aunt to me. As she can never resist the temptation of cheesecake, this is a special recipe which I made for her.

175g / 6oz digestive biscuits
75g / 3oz butter
225g / 8oz cottage cheese
50g / 2oz caster sugar
juice and grated rind of 1 lemon
275ml / ½ pint double cream
lemon slices, grated lemon rind or grapes to decorate

1. Crush the biscuits. Melt the butter and mix in the biscuit crumbs.
2. Cover the base of a 18cm / 7in flan dish with the crumb mixture, and chill for 10 minutes in the fridge.
3. Whip the cream till it is stiff. Lightly mix together the cottage cheese, caster sugar, lemon rind and juice. Fold in the cream.

4. Spread this mixture over the biscuit base. Decorate with half slices of fresh lemon or grapes cut in half (remember to remove the pips). You can also sprinkle grated lemon rind on top – it's mouth-watering!

My pavlova

The delicious pavlova comes from Australia, and was named after the great Russian ballerina Anna Pavlova when she visited that continent. It consists of a mixture of cream and fruit in a meringue case.

Cooking time: 1 hour

4 egg whites
175g / 6oz caster sugar
1 level teaspoon cornflour
1 teaspoon raspberry vinegar
275ml / ½ pint whipping cream
18 fresh strawberries, cut in half
1 kiwi fruit, peeled and thinly sliced

1. Pre-heat the oven to 170°C / 325°F or gas mark 3. Line a baking sheet with baking parchment, mark out a circle of 20cm / 8in diameter with a cake tin.
2. Beat or whisk the egg whites in a large bowl until stiff. Now add the sugar 1 teaspoon at a time, beating the mixture continuously. It will soon become thick and glossy.
3. Mix the last teaspoon of sugar with the raspberry vinegar and cornflour, making sure that it is mixed really well. Pour this into the egg whites and whisk or beat thoroughly.
4. Spoon the meringue mixture onto the circle on the prepared baking sheet, building it up at the edges. Then, using a pallet knife in a light dabbing movement, pull the meringue up lightly to form soft peaks.

5. Turn the oven down to 150°C / 300°F or gas mark 2 and place the meringue in the oven. Cook for 1 hour, but do not open the door of the oven while it is cooking, even to peep, otherwise it will go flat!

6. After an hour turn the oven off, but leave the meringue inside to cool for about another hour because it will crack easily if it cools too fast.

7. Peel away the baking parchment from the pavlova when it is absolutely cold.

8. Not more than half an hour before you want to serve the pavlova, place it on an attractive-looking serving dish and spoon in some of the whipped cream, strawberries and sliced kiwi fruit. Then add the rest of the whipped cream and decorate with the remaining strawberries and kiwi fruit slices.

Chestnut dessert

425g / 15oz tin of unsweetened chestnut purée
250ml / 10fl.oz Greek yoghurt
grated rind and juice of 1 orange
1 dessertspoon clear honey
2 egg whites
grated plain chocolate or carob bar to decorate

1. Put the chestnut purée and the yoghurt in a bowl and beat thoroughly. Add the orange rind, juice and honey and beat again.

2. Whisk the egg whites until really stiff, then stir 2 spoonfuls into the mixture. Fold in the remaining egg white.

3. Carefully spoon into 4 tall glasses and chill for 1½ hours.

4. Serve topped with grated chocolate or carob.

Tropical cocktail lollies

My friends and I used to make these really delicious lollies on hot summer days.

575ml / 1 pint yoghurt, any flavour
225g / 8oz tin of fruit cocktail

1. Put the yoghurt in a bowl, stir until it is smooth.
2. Drain the fruit cocktail and stir into the yoghurt.
3. Spoon the mixture into lollypop moulds or paper cups, putting a lolly stick in the centre of each cup.
4. Freeze until firm, about 2-3 hours.

Blackberry delight

Cooking time: 20 minutes

450g / 1lb blackberries, washed
juice of 1 lemon
2 egg whites, whipped
25g / 1oz powdered agar agar
110g / 4oz caster sugar
3 tablespoons cold water
150ml / $\frac{1}{4}$ pint double cream, whipped
cream to serve

1. Cook the blackberries over a low heat with the lemon juice till soft. Add the sugar, cover and simmer for 5 minutes.
2. Put the water in a basin and sprinkle the agar agar in. Leave for 5 minutes.
3. Remove the blackberries from the heat and stir in the agar agar.
4. Press the fruit through a sieve into a bowl, discarding all pips etc. Leave to cool and then fold in first the whipped cream, then the whipped egg whites.

5. Carefully spoon into tall glasses and allow to set, then serve with cream on top.

Banana split (for one)

1 medium-sized banana
1 scoop each of 3 different ice creams
25g / 1oz walnuts, chopped
3 cherries (glacé or maraschino)
65ml / 2½fl.oz whipping cream, whipped
chocolate sauce
1 wafer, cut in half diagonally

1. Split the banana in half lengthwise. Put 3 scoops of ice cream in a row in a shallow oval dish and place the banana halves on either side.
2. Sprinkle a few of the chopped walnuts over the ice cream, then pour over the chocolate sauce.
3. Pipe or spoon the whipped cream over the ice cream and a little on each side of the banana. Sprinkle the rest of the nuts over the cream and decorate with the cherries and wafers. Serve at once.

Summer day favourite

1 tablespoon clear honey
225g / 8oz fresh strawberries, hulled
275ml / ½ pint cold water
225g / 8oz chopped cashew nuts

1. Mix the water and cashew nuts in a liquidiser.
2. Then add the honey and strawberries and mix again till fairly smooth.

3. Pour into a suitable container (such as one you keep ice cream in) and then put into a freezer until completely solid.
4. Take out of the freezer at least 10 to 15 minutes before serving.

Paradise

This is a rich dessert for special occasions.

275ml / ½ pint milk
150ml / ¼ pint Greek yoghurt, chilled
150ml / ¼ pint whipping cream, chilled
1 tablespoon custard powder
225g / 8oz fresh or defrosted summer fruits
3 tablespoons caster sugar
grated carob or chopped nuts to decorate

1. Mix the custard powder and caster sugar to a smooth paste with 3 tablespoons of milk.
2. Heat the rest of the milk in a saucepan until it just comes to the boil. Take the saucepan off the stove and slowly stir the milk into the custard paste. Leave to get cold.
3. Whip the cream till it is stiff. Fold the fruit and cream into the custard, then the yoghurt.
4. Spoon into 4 tall glasses and decorate with grated carob or chopped nuts.

Strawberry delight

450g / 1lb strawberries
225g / 8oz raspberries
juice of 1 orange
1 tablespoonful light brown sugar

1. Wash and quarter the strawberries and put in a serving dish. Chill.

2. Put the raspberries, orange juice and sugar into a liquidiser and blend until smooth.

3. Spoon this sauce over the strawberries and serve.

Brown Bettie's ice cream

50g / 2oz chopped hazelnuts
75g / 3oz brown breadcrumbs
50g / 2oz granulated sugar
3 egg whites
75g / 3oz soft brown sugar
275ml / ½ pint whipping cream

1. Put the chopped nuts, breadcrumbs and granulated sugar in a small baking tin and place under a pre-heated grill, stirring occasionally, until the sugar has melted and the breadcrumbs have caramelised. Set aside to cool completely.

2. Whisk the egg whites until stiff, then carefully fold in the brown sugar.

3. In a separate bowl whisk the whipping cream and spoon this very carefully into the egg white mixture. Now fold in the nuts and breadcrumbs.

4. Spoon the ingredients into a suitable container and put in the freezer for a few hours until set.

When serving the ice cream, remove it from the freezer and place it in the refrigerator for about 20 minutes so it softens slightly.

Homemade yoghurt

There is nothing quite like homemade yoghurt, which is actually far better for you than much that is sold in shops and supermarkets. Yoghurt sold in shops often has artificial colouring and flavourings. So it is certainly worthwhile making your own and it is really quite simple.

Depending upon the kind of yoghurt you want you can use skimmed milk to make a low-fat yoghurt or full fat milk to make yoghurt with a more creamy flavour. Long-life milk is easiest to use as you do not need to boil it. If you use pasteurised fresh milk this has to be boiled and then cooled to about 37°C before making the yoghurt.

When preparing homemade yoghurt make sure that you buy natural yoghurt that has not been pasteurised and is not of the long-life kind.

575ml / 1 pint long-life milk
1 tablespoon natural yoghurt
2 tablespoons skimmed milk powder

1. Sterilise a thermos flask with boiling water, which will also warm it.
2. Heat the milk on the stove to 37°C.
3. Put the yoghurt in a basin with the skimmed milk powder, pour on a little warm milk, stir thoroughly. Pour this mixture into the warmed flask and add the rest of the milk.
4. Seal the flask and leave overnight to set.

Marshmallow spice ice cream

This tastes like rich frozen fudge.

110g / 4oz marshmallows
1 large tin of evaporated milk
2 teaspoons ground cinnamon

110g / 4oz soft dark brown sugar
150-225ml / 5-8fl.oz double or whipping cream

1. Melt the marshmallows gently in a pan with the evaporated milk, the cinnamon and the sugar, stirring all the time until smooth. Transfer to a bowl to cool.
2. Whisk the cream until thick but not stiff and fold thoroughly into the marshmallow mixture.
3. Transfer to a suitable container and freeze for at least 3 hours.

Apple fool

450g / 1lb cooking apples
50g / 2oz sugar
2 egg whites
110-150g / 4-5oz double cream

1. Peel and core the apples and slice thinly.
2. Put into a pan with the sugar and a dessertspoon of water and simmer very gently, stirring now and again, until the apples turn to pulp. Remove from the heat and cool.
3. Whisk the egg whites until really stiff and whisk the cream a little.
4. Fold the egg whites into the apple and gently stir in the cream.
5. Leave in the fridge to set.

Macaroni applecake

175g / 6oz ginger nuts or digestive biscuits, crushed
75g / 3oz margarine, melted
2 425g / 15oz tins of creamed macaroni
grated rind and juice of 1 lemon

2 dessert apples, peeled, cored and grated
¹/₂ teaspoon mixed spice
50g / 2oz caster sugar
150ml / ¹/₄ pint whipped cream
1 red apple, cored and thinly sliced

1. Mix the biscuit crumbs with the melted margarine.
2. Combine the creamed macaroni with the lemon rind, grated apple, mixed spice and sugar.
3. Put half the macaroni mixture into a glass bowl and cover with most of the crumb mixture and then the remaining macaroni. Sprinkle with the rest of the crumb mixture and pipe or spoon the whipped cream on top.
4. Chill for at least 30 minutes. Serve the applecake decorated with apple slices sprinkled with lemon juice to prevent discoloration.

Vanilla apricot crunch

400g / 14oz tin of apricots in natural juice
25g / 1oz walnuts, chopped finely
40g / 1¹/₂oz margarine
50g / 2oz fresh brown breadcrumbs
2 level tablespoons granulated sugar
pinch of ground cinnamon
vanilla ice cream

1. Blend the apricots and juice until smooth.
2. Melt the margarine in a frying pan, add the breadcrumbs, nuts, sugar and cinnamon and cook over a moderate heat, stirring occasionally, until this mixture is brown and crisp.
3. Put scoops of ice cream in individual dishes, scatter the crumbs, hot or cold, over the top and pour the apricot sauce round.

Cakes and confectionery

Carrot crazy

Cooking time: 1 hour

175g / 6oz stoned dates
125ml / 4fl.oz water
175g / 6oz margarine
2 large eggs
225g / 8oz self-raising flour
200g / 7oz carrots, peeled and finely grated
40g / 1$\frac{1}{2}$oz ground almonds
grated rind of 1 orange
$\frac{1}{2}$ teaspoon ground ginger
$\frac{1}{2}$ teaspoon ground cinnamon
$\frac{1}{2}$ teaspoon mixed spice

icing and filling:
225g / 8oz quark
25g / 1oz margarine
grated rind of 1 orange
cinnamon, or grated carrot and chopped walnuts to decorate

1. Simmer the dates in the water for 12-15 minutes, then chop finely. Keep the liquid.

2. Cream the butter or margarine with the liquid in which the eggs and the dates simmered.

3. Lightly but thoroughly fold in all the remaining ingredients.

4. Oil an 20cm / 8in square cake tin. Spoon the mixture into this and bake in the oven at 180°C / 350°F or gas mark 4 for 1 hour or until cooked.

5. Allow the cake to cook in the tin for 10 minutes, then turn out onto a wire rack and leave until cold.

6. Beat the quark, margarine and orange rind well together. Cut the cake in half horizontally, spread most of the mixture over the cake and sandwich together. Cover the top of the cake with the remaining icing and sprinkle with ground cinnamon or grated carrots and chopped walnuts.

No egg fruit cake

Cooking time: 30-35 minutes

225g / 8oz self-raising flour
50g / 2oz margarine
110g / 4oz dried fruit (any kind)
110g / 4oz sugar
50g / 2oz chopped peel
$^1/_2$ teaspoon bicarbonate of soda
1 tablespoon vinegar
150ml / $^1/_4$ pint milk or soya milk

1. Sieve the flour into a large bowl, add the margarine and rub in with your fingertips till it resembles fine breadcrumbs.

2. Add the sugar, fruit and peel and stir in with a wooden spoon.

3. Put the milk into a jug together with the vinegar and bicarbonate of soda and stir well with a spoon. Pour into the other ingredients and stir till smooth.

4. Spoon or pour the mixture into a greased square shallow tin lined with baking parchment. Place the tin in the middle of the oven and cook at 180°C / 350°F or gas mark 4 for about 30-35 minutes until it is firm to the touch. (Press a finger gently onto the cake – if it springs back, it is done.)
5. Allow the cake to cool in the tin for a whole, then turn it out onto a wire rack. Leave to get cold.

'Chocolate' carob cake

Cooking time: 30-45 minutes

50g / 2oz self-raising flour
75g / 3oz granary flour
50g / 2oz carob powder
10g / ¹/₂oz porridge oats
10g / ¹/₂oz desiccated coconut
175g / 6oz margarine
175g / 6oz soft brown sugar
3 lightly beaten eggs
1 level teaspoon baking powder
grated rind and 1 tablespoon juice from 1 orange

1. Grease a 20cm / 8in cake tin and line it with greaseproof paper.
2. Sieve all the dry ingredients together into a bowl. In a separate bowl cream the margarine and sugar until light and fluffy.
3. Next, gradually add the sieved ingredients and the beaten eggs to the creamed margarine and sugar, then add the orange rind and one tablespoon of juice.
4. Pour the cake mixture into the prepared tin and bake at 160°C / 325°F or gas mark 3 for 30-45 minutes or until firm when touched.

A very attractive crunchy topping can be obtained if some brown sugar is sprinkled over the cake before baking.

An old family cake recipe

Cooking time: 35-40 minutes

base:
175g / 6oz margarine
225g / 8oz plain flour
75g / 3oz granulated sugar
1 teaspoon ground ginger

topping:
1 teaspoon ground ginger
1 tablespoon syrup
2 tablespoons icing sugar
50g / 2oz margarine

1. Sieve the flour and ginger into a bowl, then add the granulated sugar and mix them all together.
2. Add the margarine and rub in with your fingers until you can form it into a ball.
3. Put the mixture in a Swiss roll tin and press down lightly with a palette knife.
4. Place in the middle of the oven and bake at 180°C / 350°F or gas mark 4 for 35-40 minutes. It should still be slightly soft. Turn out onto a wire rack to cool.
5. Meanwhile make the topping. Put the margarine and syrup in a saucepan and melt over a gentle heat. Add the icing sugar and ginger and stir in thoroughly. Then remove from the heat.
6. Pour the topping onto the base while still warm. Smooth with a palette knife.
7. Now you can cut it into medium-sized fingers to serve.

Liquid is not required for the base.

Wholemeal chocolate cake

Cooking time: 30-35 minutes

175g / 6oz wholemeal flour
110g / 4oz margarine
110g / 4oz caster sugar
2 eggs
1¹/₂ teaspoons baking powder
1 tablespoon cocoa powder
1 tablespoon milk

filling and topping:
75g / 3oz margarine
110g / 4oz icing sugar
few drops pure vanilla essence
melted chocolate
walnut halves to decorate

1. Cream the margarine with the sugar until light and fluffy.
2. Beat the eggs in one at a time until the mixture is smooth.
3. Sieve the flour, baking powder and cocoa into the bowl and fold in. Add the milk and stir very lightly, but try not to let too much air out of the cake mixture.
4. Grease two 15cm / 6in sandwich tins and line with baking parchment. Divide the cake mixture evenly between the tins.
5. Bake in the oven at 190°C / 375°F or gas mark 5 for 30-35 minutes until well risen. Leave the sponges to cool slightly in the tins before putting them on a rack to cool.
6. Make the filling by creaming the margarine well. Add the icing sugar a little at a time, finally add the vanilla essence. Beat until creamy.
7. Sandwich the sponges together with the filling. Cover the top of the sponge with melted chocolate, decorate with some walnut halves.

Apfelkuchen

This is based on a traditional German recipe, but it is a low sugar version. It can be served hot or cold.

Cooking time: 35-40 minutes

275g / 10oz wholewheat flour
225g / 8oz margarine
2 eggs
2 teaspoons baking powder
50g / 2oz sultanas
1 teaspoon ground cinnamon
50g / 2oz chopped flaked almonds
2 tablespoons honey
450g / 1lb dessert apples, peeled, cored and thinly sliced
1 tablespoon concentrated apple juice
25g / 1oz flaked almonds to decorate

1. Put the sultanas, sliced apples, chopped almonds, cinnamon and apple juice in a bowl and mix with a wooden spoon.
2. Cream the margarine and honey in another bowl till light and fluffy. Add the baking powder and flour and stir in well. Finally beat in the eggs one by one.
3. Grease a 18cm / 7in round or square cake tin. Spoon half the mixture into the tin, then add the fruit, making sure it is spread evenly. Put the remaining cake mixture over the top.
4. Sprinkle with the flaked almonds and bake in the oven at 180°C / 350°F or gas mark 4 for 35-40 minutes, until the cake becomes a lovely golden-brown colour. Leave the cake in the tin on a wire rack to cool.

Orange blossom cake

Cooking time: 55-60 minutes

225g / ½lb plain wholemeal flour
110g / 4oz raw cane sugar
175g / 6oz margarine
1 egg
2 teaspoons baking powder
4 tablespoons fresh orange juice
1 tablespoon grated orange peel
3 tablespoons sugar-free marmalade

1. Cream the margarine with the sugar, then beat in the egg.
2. Stir in the marmalade, orange peel and orange juice. Then add the sieved flour and baking powder and mix to a soft dropping consistency.
3. Grease an 18-20cm / 7-8in round or square cake tin and line with baking parchment. Spoon the cake mixture into the tin, place in the centre of the oven and bake at 180°C / 350°F or gas mark 4 for 55 to 60 minutes.

This cake is delicious as it is, but if you like you can cover the top with orange glacé icing:-

Mix 1 tablespoon of fresh orange juice, 100g / 4oz sieved icing sugar and 1 tablespoon of grated orange peel very well till smooth. Spread over the top of the cake once it is cold.

Yoghurt cake

Cooking time: 40-45 minutes

150ml / 5fl.oz carton of natural yoghurt
5 cartons self-raising flour
2 cartons cooking oil
3 cartons caster sugar

3 eggs
grated rind and juice of 2 lemons

1. Put the yoghurt into a bowl. Wash and dry the yoghurt carton and use this to measure the flour and sugar, then the oil. Stir thoroughly into the yoghurt, add the eggs and the lemon rind and juice.

2. Grease a 900g / 2lb loaf tin. Pour in the mixture and bake at 200°C / 400°F or gas mark 6 for 40 to 45 minutes, until firm to the touch. Cool on a wire rack.

This makes a delicious moist madeira-type cake.

Rocky road cake

Cooking time: 25-30 minutes

50g / 2oz sultanas
50g / 2oz currants
225g / 8oz self-raising flour
$\frac{1}{2}$ teaspoon mixed spice
10g / $\frac{1}{2}$oz chopped peel
75g / 3oz white vegetable fat
$\frac{1}{4}$ teaspoon salt
little milk for mixing
75g / 3oz sugar

1. Prepare an 18cm / 7in shallow cake tin by greasing and lining with baking parchment. The tin must not be less than 5cm deep.

2. Sieve the flour into a large bowl, rub in the fat till the mixture looks like fine breadcrumbs.

3. Add the sultanas, currants, peel, mixed spice and salt and mix in thoroughly. Pour in some milk a few drops at a time, and stir till the cake mixture sticks together. When mixed it will feel sticky.

4. Spoon the mixture into the prepared cake tin, put in the middle of the oven and bake at 230°C / 450°F or gas mark 8 for 25-30 minutes until a lovely golden-brown colour.
5. Remove from the oven and sprinkle a little sugar over the top of the cake. Leave in the tin for about 10 minutes, then turn out and place on a wire rack.

Éclairs

Cooking time: 18-20 minutes

Makes: 8-10

150ml / ¼ pint whipping cream or double cream, whipped

choux pastry:
150ml / ¼ pint water
50g / 2oz margarine
110g / 4oz self-raising flour, sieved
3 eggs

chocolate glacé icing:
110g / 4oz icing sugar
1 tablespoon warm water
1 dessertspoon cocoa powder

1. Put the water and margarine in saucepan and melt over a gentle heat, then bring to the boil.
2. Remove the pan from the heat and stir in the sieved flour, return to the stove and stirring all the time cook for 1 minute or until the dough comes away from the sides of the pan and forms a ball in the middle.
3. Remove from the heat and allow to cool. Lightly beat the eggs and with a wooden spoon beat little by little into the cooled mixture until the eggs are incorporated and the pastry is soft, glistening and smooth.

4. Grease a baking tray, then hold it under the cold tap, leaving a film of water on the tray.

5. Place the choux pastry into a piping bag fitted with a plain 1cm / ½in nozzle and pipe 7cm / 3in lengths on the baking tray, making sure they are well apart as the pastry expands during cooking. Bake in a hot oven at 220°C / 425°F or gas mark 7 for 18-20 minutes.

6. Make a slit down one side of each éclair and leave them to cool on a wire rack while making the icing.

7. Sieve the icing sugar and cocoa into a bowl, add the water and stir well until smooth.

8. Fill the éclairs with whipped cream and coat the top with the chocolate glacé icing.

Jam or lemon curd tarts

Cooking time: 12-15 minutes

Makes: 12

225g / 8oz self-raising flour
50g / 2oz margarine
50g / 2oz white vegetable fat
25g / 1oz caster sugar
2 tablespoons cold water
jam or lemon curd

1. Sieve the flour into a bowl, add margarine and fat and rub into the flour until the mixture resembles fine breadcrumbs. Sprinkle the water over the mixture and stir with the blade of a knife till a stiff dough is formed. If necessary knead briefly.

2. Roll the pastry out thinly on a lightly floured surface, cut out rounds with a pastry cutter and use these to line patty tins.

3. Put a little jam or lemon curd in each but make very sure you do not overfill.

4. Bake in the oven at 200°C / 400°F or gas mark 6 for 12-15 minutes.

Banana cake

Cooking time: 20-25 minutes

4 tablespoons oil
25g / 1oz molasses
50g / 2oz honey
2 eggs
2 bananas, mashed
110g / 4oz chopped walnuts
110g / 4oz flour
2 teaspoons baking powder

1. Cream the oil, molasses and honey together until light and fluffy.
2. One at a time, beat in the eggs, adding 1 tablespoon of flour with the second egg. Then fold in the rest of the flour with the baking powder and the bananas.
3. Spoon the cake mixture into a greased and lined 20cm / 8in square shallow tin, smooth the top. Scatter the walnuts over the top and then bake in the oven at 190°C / 375°F or gas mark 5 for 20-25 minutes until the cake springs back when pressed gently.
4. Leave in the tin for a few minutes, then turn out and allow to cool on a wire rack.

Fruit bread

Cooking time: 70-75 minutes

50g / 2oz chopped walnuts
110g / 4oz soft brown sugar
110g / 4oz margarine, softened
110g / 4oz sultanas
2 large eggs
1 large cooking apple, peeled, cored and chopped
1 tablespoon honey
175g / 6oz self-raising flour
50g / 2oz wholemeal flour
1 teaspoon mixed spice
pinch of salt

1. Grease one 900g / 2lb or two 450g / 1lb loaf tins and line with baking parchment.
2. Put all the ingredients in a large bowl and beat thoroughly for about 2 minutes.
3. Spoon the mixture into the prepared tin(s) and bake at 180°C / 350°F or gas mark 4 for one hour, then reduce the heat to 160°C / 325°F or gas mark 3 for a further 10-15 minutes.
4. Allow to cool in the tin(s), then turn out onto a wire rack.

This is delicious when sliced, with jam or just butter!

Mitzi's delight

Cooking time: 30-35 minutes

110g / 4oz chocolate chips (plain or milk)
175g / 6oz plain flour
$1/2$ teaspoon baking powder
110g / 4oz margarine
110g / 4oz sugar

2 eggs, beaten
a little milk

filling:
50g / 2oz margarine
110g / 4oz sieved icing sugar

1. Cream the margarine and sugar till light and fluffy. Add the chocolate chips and stir in well.
2. Then add the eggs a little at a time, beating well after each addition.
3. Fold in the sieved flour and baking powder and add a little milk to give a soft dropping consistency.
4. Divide the cake mixture between two 18cm / 7in greased cake tins and bake in the oven at 190°C / 375°F or gas mark 5 for 30-35 minutes until golden-brown and firm to the touch.
5. Turn out onto a wire rack to get cold. Meanwhile cream the margarine in a bowl and gradually add the sieved icing sugar, beat till light and fluffy.
6. Sandwich the two sponges together with this filling and dust the top of the cake with a little sieved icing sugar.

Apple spice slab

Cooking time: 30 minutes

110g / 4oz margarine
60g / 2½oz light brown sugar
2 tablespoons clear honey
225g / 8oz oats
1 large cooking apple, peeled, cored and thinly sliced
1 teaspoon cinnamon

1. Put 50g / 2oz of the sugar and the honey in a saucepan and heat gently, stirring until melted. Stir in the oats.

2. Spread half the mixture in a greased 18cm / 7in tin and arrange the apple slices on top. Sprinkle the rest of the oats mixture over the apple, then the remaining sugar and the cinnamon.

3. Bake in the oven at 190°C / 375°F or gas mark 5 for 30 minutes until golden and crisp. Remove from the oven and cut into slices while still hot, but leave to cool in the tin.

Lemon cake

Cooking time: 15-20 minutes

175g / 6oz margarine
175g / 6oz light or dark brown sugar
2 large eggs
225g / 8oz self-raising flour
grated rind of 1 lemon

icing:
juice of 1 lemon
75g / 3oz caster sugar

1. Cream the margarine in a bowl, beat in the eggs.
2. Fold in the flour and the lemon rind.
3. Grease a 18 x 25cm / 7 x 10in cake tin and spoon in the cake mixture. Bake for 15-20 minutes at 180°C / 350°F or gas mark 4.
4. Mix the lemon juice and caster sugar well and pour over the top of the cake immediately you take it from the oven.

No bake chocolate fudge cake

225g / 8oz plain chocolate
450g / 1lb digestive biscuits
75g / 3oz caster sugar
1 teaspoon instant coffee powder
50g / 2oz glacé cherries, chopped
50g / 2oz walnuts, chopped
50g / 2oz margarine
210g / 7½oz tin of evaporated milk
2 eggs, beaten

1. Break the chocolate into small pieces, place in a basin over a saucepan of hot water, leave until melted.

2. Put the biscuits into a polythene bag and crush them well with a rolling pin. Empty them into a bowl with the sugar and the coffee powder, cherries and walnuts.

3. Heat the margarine and evaporated milk slowly in a saucepan until the margarine melts. Take off the heat, add the chocolate, and gradually stir in the eggs.

4. Pour onto the crumb mixture and stir until thoroughly mixed.

5. Transfer to a greased and lined baking tin and smooth the top with a knife.

6. Chill overnight, then turn out and cut into slices.

Gran's chocolate crunch

If you are looking for something special to make, then this is for you!

110g / 4oz margarine
2 tablespoons golden syrup
150g / 5oz plain chocolate
225g / 8oz plain sweet biscuits, crushed
75g / 3oz glacé cherries, roughly chopped
50g / 2oz raisins
50g / 2oz chopped candied peel
1 rounded teaspoon ground cinnamon

icing:
2 heaped tablespoons icing sugar
2 teaspoons warm water
glacé cherries to decorate

1. Slowly melt the margarine, golden syrup and chocolate in a saucepan. When smooth, stir in the rest of the ingredients.

2. Spoon the mixture into a lightly oiled, small loaf or cake tin and smooth the top. Leave to cool and then chill in the refrigerator. When it is chilled turn the cake onto a serving dish.
3. Stir the icing sugar and water together until smooth and spread over the top of the cake, letting it dribble down the sides. Decorate with halved or chopped glacé cherries.
4. Chill once more. Cut into thin slices and serve with or without cream. It is especially delicious with vanilla ice cream!

Victoria sandwich

Cooking time: 20-25 minutes

110g / 4oz margarine
110g / 4oz caster sugar
110g / 4oz self-raising flour
2 eggs

1. Cream the margarine and sugar until light and fluffy.
2. Beat in the eggs one at a time, adding a little flour with each egg.
3. Divide the cake mixture between two greased 15cm / 6in sandwich tins and bake in a moderate oven at 180°C / 350°F or gas mark 4 for 20-25 minutes or until golden-brown.
4. Turn the sponges onto a wire rack to cool. When cold, sandwich together with jam or fresh cream and dust the top of the cake with icing sugar.

Chocolate mint creams

Makes: about 20

1 egg white
225g / 8oz icing sugar, sieved
1 teaspoon peppermint essence
few drops of green and red food colouring
225g / 8oz milk or plain cooking chocolate

1. Put the egg white into a bowl and gradually stir in 6oz of
icing sugar until the mixture is stiff, knead in the rest of the
icing sugar to form a firm paste. Add peppermint essence to
taste.
2. Divide the mixture into three pieces, add a few drops of
green food colouring to one, red food colouring to another,
leaving the remaining piece plain white.
3. Dust a board with icing sugar and roll out each piece of
sugar paste thinly to just over ¹/₂cm. Cut into 3¹/₂cm / 1¹/₂in
fluted rounds, using a biscuit cutter.
4. Leave to dry overnight on greaseproof paper.
5. Melt the chocolate in a bowl over a pan of hot water. Dip
half of each peppermint cream only into the melted chocolate
and leave on a wire rack to set.

Marshmallow pyramids

25g / 1oz marshmallows
25g / 1oz vanilla fudge
5g / ¹/₄oz margarine
40g / 1¹/₂oz cornflakes

1. Heat the marshmallows, fudge and margarine in a
saucepan over a very low heat.
2. Cool, then stir in the cornflakes.

3. Form into pyramid shapes, and leave on greaseproof paper to set.

Sugar mice

Makes: 8

450g / 1lb icing sugar
1 egg white, lightly beaten
50g / 2oz golden syrup
few drops of pink food colouring
2 sticks liquorice
16 silver balls

1. Sieve three quarters of the icing sugar into a bowl. Add the egg white and syrup and mix well. Gradually knead in the remaining icing sugar.
2. Add a few drops of pink food colouring and knead well until the fondant is smooth and evenly coloured.
3. Cut off a small piece and reserve for making ears. Divide the remaining mixture equally into 8 pieces and shape each piece into a round ball, then press one end to a point to form the head and nose of the mouse. Leave the other end rounded.
4. Shape the reserved piece of fondant into 16 ears. Press 2 ears firmly onto the head of each mouse and press silver balls into each face for eyes.
5. Cut the sticks of liquorice into 8 strips and use to make tails.

Keep the sugar mice in a tin so that they do not become too hard.

Naughty but nice chocolates

These chocolates will make a very special present for someone you care about.

Makes: 14-15

50ml / 2fl.oz double cream
110g / 4oz plain chocolate
1 tablespoon rum
cocoa powder or desiccated coconut

1. Break the chocolate into small pieces and melt in a bowl over a pan of hot water.
2. When melted, stir the rum in thoroughly and let the mixture cool completely.

3. Whisk the double cream until it becomes light and fluffy, and carefully fold it into the cold chocolate / rum mixture.
4. Form into balls the size of a walnut with your fingers and roll these in cocoa powder or desiccated coconut.
5. Put the chocolates in petit four cases on a small tray and chill for 30 minutes.

Biscuits and scones

Boston brownies

Cooking time: 15 minutes

Makes: 14-16

75g / 3oz plain carob bar
50g / 2oz margarine
110g / 4oz light muscovado sugar
1 egg
25g / 1oz plain wholemeal flour
50g / 2oz plain flour
1/2 teaspoon baking powder
1 teaspoon vanilla essence
1/2 teaspoon salt
50g / 2oz walnuts, chopped

1. Break the carob bar into pieces and put into a bowl with the margarine and sugar. Place the bowl over a pan of boiling water until the carob melts. Make sure no water gets into the bowl.
2. Sieve the flours and baking powder together and add any bran left in the sieve.
3. Now very thoroughly mix all ingredients.
4. Spoon the brownie mixture into a lightly greased and lined 20cm / 7in square cake tin and spread evenly.
5. Bake at 180°C / 350°F or gas mark 4 for 15 minutes, until slightly risen and shiny on top.
6. Remove from the oven, allow to cool in the tin and cut into squares. Keep in an airtight container.

Sylvia's rocky mountains

Cooking time: 15-20 minutes

225g / 8oz self-raising flour
pinch of salt
110g / 4oz margarine
75g / 3oz currants
110g / 4oz sugar
50g / 2oz mixed peel
3 eggs
milk to mix

1. Mix the flour and salt, rub in the margarine.
2. Stir in the sugar, currants and peel and mix in the egg.
Gradually add a few drops of milk, to form a stiff dough.
3. Place in rough heaps on a greased baking tray and bake in
the oven at 200°C / 400°F or gas mark 6 for 15-20 minutes.

Veronica's flapjacks

Cooking time: 30-35 minutes

Makes: 8-10

1 teaspoon fresh lemon juice
225g / 8oz porridge oats
75g / 3oz demerara sugar
1 tablespoon golden syrup
150g / 5oz margarine
pinch of salt

1. Melt the sugar, margarine and syrup in a saucepan over a
gentle heat until the sugar has dissolved.
2. Remove from the heat, add the lemon juice, salt and
porridge oats and stir well.

3. Spoon the flapjack mixture into a greased 18cm / 7in shallow cake tin and bake in the oven at 190°C / 375°F or gas mark 5 for 30-35 minutes.

4. Remove the tin from the oven, place it on a wire rack and cut the flapjacks into slices while still warm. Allow to go cold in the tin.

Demelza's cookies

Cooking time: 15 minutes

Makes: 18

225g / 8oz roasted peanuts
25g / 1oz porridge oats
1 teaspoon bicarbonate of soda
75g / 3oz light muscovado sugar
75g / 3oz plain carob chips
1 tablespoon clear honey
50g / 2oz margarine
1 egg, beaten

1. Put the peanuts into a blender and chop until they are very fine and just starting to blend together.

2. Mix the peanuts, oats, bicarbonate of soda, sugar and carob chips in a bowl.

3. Melt the honey and margarine in a saucepan and stir into the dry ingredients together with the egg.

4. Drop small amounts of the mixture onto a lightly greased baking sheet, leaving about 8cm between each cookie for spreading.

5. Bake in the oven at 180°C / 350°F or gas mark 4 for 15 minutes until the cookies are golden-brown and beginning to harden around the edge. Leave to cool for about 5 minutes on the baking sheet, then transfer to a wire rack to cool completely.

Health bars

Cooking time: 25-28 minutes

175g / 6oz jumbo oats
25g / 1oz sesame seeds
25g / 1oz muscovado sugar
6 tablespoons clear honey
25g / 1oz desiccated coconut
50g / 2oz sunflower seeds
4 tablespoons vegetable oil
50g / 2oz sultanas
50g / 2oz raisins

1. Gently heat the honey and oil in a saucepan on the stove
until the honey has melted, stirring all the time.
2. Mix all other ingredients in a large mixing bowl and pour in
the honey and oil, stirring all the time so that all the
ingredients are coated.
3. Spoon the mixture into a greased baking tin and press
down with a palette knife until it is level on top.
4. Place in the oven at 180°C / 350°F or gas mark 4 for 25-28
minutes until it turns a lovely golden colour.
5. Put the tin on a wire rack to cool slightly. Cut into bars,
remove from the tin and leave on a wire rack to go cold. Store
in an airtight tin.

Wholemeal yoghurt scones

Cooking time: 7-10 minutes

Makes: 12-15

225g / 8oz wholemeal flour
1 teaspoon salt
1 teaspoon bicarbonate of soda
25g / 1oz margarine
150ml / 4fl.oz natural yoghurt
few drops of milk

1. Put the flour, salt and bicarbonate of soda in a bowl, rub in the margarine and stir in the yoghurt to make a soft, not sticky, dough.
2. Roll out to 1cm / ½in thick on a lightly floured surface and cut into rounds, using a 5cm / 2in plain cutter.
3. Place on a greased baking sheet and brush the tops of the scones with a little milk.
4. Bake in the oven for 7-10 minutes at 220°C / 425°F or gas mark 7 until well risen and golden.
5. Leave on a wire rack to cool.

Ron's flapjacks

Cooking time: 18-20 minutes

110g / 4oz margarine
1 tablespoon golden syrup
110g / 4oz sugar
50g / 2oz oats
50g / 2oz self-raising flour
75g / 3oz crushed cornflakes

1. Melt the margarine and syrup very gently in a saucepan on the stove.
2. Mix the dry ingredients in a bowl, then pour on the margarine and syrup and mix well.
3. Spread the mixture evenly in a greased Swiss roll tin and press down firmly.
4. Bake in the oven at 190°C / 375°F or gas mark 5 for 18-20 minutes.
5. Cut into fingers while still warm and allow to cool on a wire rack.

Chocolate clusters

275g / 10oz cooking chocolate or carob
200g / 7oz cornflakes

1. Break the chocolate or carob into small pieces and put in a bowl over a pan of hot water to melt.
2. When the chocolate has melted, remove the bowl from the heat and stir in the cornflakes until the mixture is quite stiff.
3. Spoon heaps into petit four cases or onto a sheet of greaseproof paper and leave to cool until set. Keep in an airtight tin.

Lavinia's crunch

Cooking time: 3-4 minutes

3 Mars bars
75g / 3oz rice crispies
25g / 1oz margarine

1. Melt the margarine in a pan. Cut the Mars bars into small pieces and add, stir until melted.

2. Next, add the rice crispies and stir thoroughly.

3. Spoon the mixture into a small greased tin, flatten the top with a knife and leave to cool. Then put it into the refrigerator until hard, and cut into pieces.

Nutty jammy dodgers

Cooking time: 12-15 minutes

Makes: 20

75g / 3oz margarine
75g / 3oz light muscovado sugar
3 tablespoons beaten egg
few drops pure vanilla essence
110g / 4oz plain flour
50g / 2oz mixed nuts, chopped
4-5 tablespoons blackcurrant jam

1. Cream the margarine with the sugar in a bowl. Add the egg and vanilla essence and beat well.

2. Add the flour and mix to form a fairly firm dough. Knead lightly until smooth.

3. Roll out the dough to about 3cm / 1¼in thick on a lightly floured surface. Cut out rounds using a 5cm / 2in fluted cutter. Cut out a small circle from the centre of half of these rounds with a 1cm / ½in fluted cutter. Re-knead and re-roll the trimmings, to make 20 rounds and 20 rings.

4. Sprinkle the rings with chopped nuts, pressing the nuts on lightly.

5. Place the rounds and rings on a lightly greased baking sheet and bake in the oven at 180°C / 350°F or gas mark 4 for 12-15 minutes. Cool on a wire rack.

6. Just before serving, spread the rounds with jam and place the nutty ring on top.

No bake chocolate slices

225g / 8oz dark chocolate
225g / 8oz margarine
75g / 3oz icing sugar, sieved
3 eggs
450g / 1lb Nice biscuits
225g / 8oz mixed walnuts, glacé cherries and raisins, chopped

1. Break up the chocolate, melt in a saucepan with the margarine over a gentle heat.
2. Remove from the heat and beat in the sugar and the eggs.
3. Crush half the biscuits, stir into the chocolate mixture, then add the nuts and fruit.
4. Put a layer of whole biscuits in the base of a small loaf tin lined with foil, cover with some of the mixture, then press another layer of biscuits on top. Continue layering until all the ingredients have been used, finishing with biscuits.
5. Leave overnight in the fridge to set.
6. Ease from the tin, peel off the foil and cut into slices.

Date slices

Cooking time: 20 minutes

110g / 4oz margarine
225g / 8oz sugar
2 eggs
1 teaspoon pure vanilla essence
75g / 3oz plain flour
1 teaspoon baking powder
175g / 6oz dates, stoned and chopped

1. Cream the margarine and sugar until light and fluffy and beat in the eggs and vanilla.

2. Sift together the flour and baking powder and stir into the mixture with the dates until all the ingredients are well blended.

3. Spoon into a greased 20cm / 8in square cake tin and bake for 20 minutes at 180°C / 350°F or gas mark 4.

4. Cut into slices while still warm, but allow to cool in the tin.

5. These slices are sticky, so do not put them on top of each other when storing.

Honey slices

Cooking time: 45-50 minutes

225g / 8oz plain flour
1 teaspoon baking powder
1 teaspoon bicarbonate of soda
1 teaspoon salt
1 teaspoon cinnamon
$1/2$ teaspoon ginger
175g / $1/2$ cup honey
1 egg, beaten
150ml / 5fl.oz milk

1. Sieve all dry ingredients together.

2. Add the beaten egg, honey and milk and beat well.

3. Allow to stand for 20 minutes, then put the mixture into a small greased loaf tin and bake in the oven at 180°C / 350°F or gas mark 4 for 45-50 minutes.

4. Keep for a day before cutting into slices and serving.

Butter leaves

Cooking time: 10 minutes

110g / 4oz butter
50g / 2oz caster sugar
1 egg, separated
200g / 7oz flour
25g / 1oz chopped nuts (walnuts, hazelnuts or almonds)
2 tablespoons granulated sugar

1. Cream the butter with the caster sugar until light and fluffy.
2. Mix in the egg yolk and the flour. Put in the fridge to chill.
3. Roll out thinly and cut into leaf shapes.
4. Put the biscuits on a greased baking sheet. Brush with beaten egg white and sprinkle with the nuts and granulated sugar.
5. Bake in a moderate oven at 180°C / 350°F or gas mark 4 for about 10 minutes.
6. Transfer to a wire rack to cool.

Gingerbread men

Cooking time: 8-10 minutes

Makes: 10

50g / 2oz margarine
75g / 3oz light muscovado sugar
2 tablespoons clear honey
110g / 4oz plain wholemeal flour
75g / 3oz plain flour
2 teaspoons ground ginger
1 teaspoon bicarbonate of soda
1 small egg, beaten
20 currants

1. Melt the margarine, honey and sugar in a saucepan over a low heat, stirring constantly until the sugar dissolves.

2. Sieve the ginger, flours and bicarbonate of soda into a bowl and make a well in the centre.

3. Pour in the melted mixture and mix thoroughly, then add the beaten egg a little at a time to form a soft dough. Let the dough stand for 5 minutes so it can cool slightly.

4. Roll out the dough on a floured surface to about ½cm / ¼in thickness and cut out the gingerbread men.

5. Put the shapes on greased baking sheets. Press currants into the dough for eyes.

6. Bake in the oven at 190°C / 375°F or gas mark 5 for 8 to 10 minutes. Carefully transfer to a wire rack and leave to cool. They will keep for up to 2 weeks in an airtight tin.

Midnight cookies

Cooking time: 10 minutes

110g / 4oz margarine
110g / 4oz soft brown sugar
2 large eggs
2 tablespoons peanut butter
50g / 2oz honey roast peanuts, chopped
50g / 2oz dried banana chips
few drops pure vanilla essence
200g / 7oz plain flour
200g / 7oz plain wholemeal flour
2 teaspoons baking powder

1. Cream the margarine with the sugar until light and fluffy. Gradually add the peanut butter and the eggs and beat well.

2. Sieve the flours and baking powder and add to the mixture. Mix thoroughly.

3. Add the vanilla essence. Stir in until the mixture resembles fine breadcrumbs. Knead gently, wrap in foil and leave for 30-40 minutes.
4. Unwrap the dough and roll it out on a floured surface to about ½cm / ¼in thick. Cut into shapes, put on a greased baking tray and sprinkle each cookie with some of the banana chips and honey roasted peanuts.
5. Bake in the oven for 10 minutes at 190°C / 375°F or gas mark 5. Put on a wire rack to cool.

Shortbread

Cooking time: 35-40 minutes

Makes: 8

110g / 4oz plain wholemeal flour
110g / 4oz plain flour
110g / 4oz ground almonds
75g / 3oz muscovado sugar
225g / 8oz margarine, softened

1. Put all the ingredients into a bowl and mix them very well to make a smooth dough.
2. Grease a 20cm / 8in loose-bottomed flat tin and press the mixture into this. Mark lightly on the top to form 8 wedges.
3. Bake in the oven for about 35-40 minutes at 160°C / 325°F or gas mark 3 until lightly golden. Cut along the markings and leave to cool in the tin.

Fruit triangles

Cooking time: 18-20 minutes

Makes: 8

225g / 8oz flour
50g / 2oz margarine
4 teaspoons baking powder
2 tablespoons cooked apple
pinch of salt
150ml / ¼ pint milk
1 egg, beaten

1. Mix the flour, baking powder and salt in a large bowl.
2. Cut the margarine into small pieces and rub into the flour till the mixture looks like fine breadcrumbs. Stir in the apple.
3. Beat the milk with the egg. Gradually stir most of this into the other ingredients to form a soft dough, but keep a little to glaze the top of the dough.
4. Knead the dough lightly on a floured surface and roll out to about 2½cm / 1in thick. Place on a lightly greased baking tray and cut across the top of the dough to form 8 triangles. Then brush the top with the remaining egg and milk mixture to glaze.
5. Place in the oven and bake at 200°C / 400°F or gas mark 6 for 18-20 minutes until risen and a lovely golden colour. Allow to cool on a wire rack.

Monster cookies

Cooking time: 15-20 minutes

Makes: 12

175g / 6oz margarine
50g / 2oz soft brown sugar
200g / 7oz crunchy peanut butter
2 tablespoons clear honey
1 egg, well beaten

2 teaspoons milk
175g / 6oz plain flour
110g / 4oz plain chocolate drops

1. Beat the margarine, peanut butter, sugar and honey with a fork in a large bowl until light and fluffy.
2. Beat in the egg and milk and fold in the sieved flour. Stir in the chocolate drops very carefully.
3. Cover the bowl with a cloth or plate and chill in the refrigerator for one hour.
4. Grease two baking sheets well. Put 4 separate tablespoons of dough onto each sheet, keeping them well separated. Use the palm of your hand to flatten each spoonful to the size of a small plate.
5. Bake in the oven at 190°C / 375°F or gas mark 5 for 15-20 minutes until they turn a nice golden-brown. Allow to cool on the baking sheets for about 5 minutes, then carefully place them on a wire rack, using a palette knife to do this.

Quick muffins

Cooking time: 20-25 minutes

Makes: 12

225g / 8oz plain flour
2 level tablespoons caster sugar
1 level tablespoon baking powder
$^1/_2$ level teaspoon salt
1 egg
225ml / 8fl.oz milk
50ml / 2fl.oz vegetable oil

1. Brush 12 muffin tins with oil or melted margarine until they are well greased.

2. Put the flour, sugar, baking powder and salt in a large bowl and stir well.

3. Beat the egg lightly with a fork in a separate bowl and then stir in the milk and oil. Add the mixture to the dry ingredients all at once and stir lightly until the flour is just moistened. Do not beat, the mixture should still be slightly lumpy.

4. Spoon the muffin dough into the greased tins, wiping off any mixture spilt on the edges. Bake in the oven at 200°C / 400°F or gas mark 6 for 20-25 minutes until well risen.

5. Serve the muffins hot, split and buttered, or allow them to cool on a wire rack and then split and toast them.

Peanut butter cookies

Cooking time: 25 minutes

Makes: 15-18

50g / 2oz crunchy peanut butter
50g / 2oz margarine
grated rind of $\frac{1}{2}$ orange
40g / $1\frac{1}{2}$oz brown sugar
50g / 2oz caster sugar
1 egg
40g / $1\frac{1}{2}$oz sultanas
110g / 4oz self-raising flour

1. Cream the peanut butter with the margarine, orange rind and sugars.

2. Beat in the egg, add the sultanas and sieved flour.

3. Roll into balls the size of a walnut and place well apart on an ungreased baking sheet.

4. Bake in a moderate oven at 180°C / 350°F or gas mark 4 for about 25 minutes. Cool on a wire rack.

Old Jack's biscuits

Cooking time: 12-15 minutes

Makes: 14

175g / 6oz margarine, softened
175g / 6oz porridge oats
75g / 3oz plain flour
1 teaspoon baking powder
pinch of salt

1. Mix all the ingredients to form a dough.
2. Roll into 14 balls and place on 2 lightly greased baking sheets. Flatten the balls with a fork, making a pattern on the top.
3. Bake at 190°C / 375°F or gas mark 5 for 12-15 minutes or until golden-brown. Cool for a few minutes on the baking sheets, then transfer to a wire rack to cool completely. Store in an airtight container.

Veronica's gingerbread

Cooking time: 45-50 minutes

225g / 8oz plain flour
$1/2$ level teaspoon bicarbonate of soda
$1/2$ level teaspoon cream of tartar
$1/2$ level teaspoon ground ginger
110g / 4oz margarine
110g / 4oz soft brown sugar
25g / 1oz crystallized ginger, chopped

1 tablespoon golden syrup
1 teaspoon granulated sugar
25g / 1oz sultanas

1. Sieve the flour, bicarbonate of soda, cream of tartar and ground ginger into a mixing bowl, add the margarine, cut into small pieces, and rub in with your fingertips until the mixture looks like fine breadcrumbs.
2. Mix in the brown sugar, chopped ginger, sultanas and syrup.
3. Press the mixture into a greased 18cm / 7in baking tin and sprinkle with granulated sugar.
4. Bake in the oven at 170°C / 325°F or gas mark 3 for 45-50 minutes. Cut into wedges and put on a wire rack to cool.

Orange crunchies

Cooking time: 18-20 minutes

1 egg, well beaten
75g / 3oz semolina
50g / 2oz margarine
110g / 4oz plain flour
50g / 2oz sugar
grated rind of 1 medium orange
$^1/_4$ teaspoon baking powder
pinch of salt
little milk for mixing

1. Sieve the flour and baking powder into a bowl and with your fingertips rub in the margarine until the mixture looks like fine breadcrumbs.
2. Add the semolina, sugar and grated orange rind and stir thoroughly.

3. Now gradually pour in the beaten egg and a little milk and mix with a wooden spoon until the dough sticks together.

4. Roll out thinly on a lightly floured surface and using a plain or fluted cutter cut out the biscuits.

5. Put them on a baking tray lined with baking parchment and bake them in the oven at 200°C / 400°F or gas mark 6 for 18-20 minutes until a lovely golden-brown. Transfer to a wire rack to cool.

Herb scones

Cooking time: 12-15 minutes

225g / 8oz self-raising flour
$^1/_2$ teaspoon salt
40g / 1$^1/_2$oz margarine
1 medium-size onion, finely chopped
50g / 2oz Edam cheese, grated
1$^1/_2$ teaspoon mixed herbs
1 egg
150ml / $^1/_4$ pint milk

1. Sieve the flour and salt into a bowl. Rub in 25g / 1oz of the margarine with your fingertips until the mixture resembles fine breadcrumbs.

2. Cook the onion in the remaining margarine until soft. Stir the onion, cheese and herbs into the flour mixture.

3. Lightly beat the egg and milk together. Keep 2 tablespoonsful separate, add the rest to the flour mixture and mix well.

4. Roll the dough out to 2cm / $^3/_4$in thick and cut into 12 rounds. Place these on a baking tray and brush the tops with the remaining egg mixture.

5. Bake at 200°C / 400°F or gas mark 6 for 12-15 minutes.

Gloria's scones

Cooking time: 15 minutes

Makes: 10-12

200g / 7oz self-raising flour
1 teaspoon salt
50g / 2oz margarine
25g / 1oz finely chopped walnuts
1 tablespoon caster sugar
1 egg, well beaten
1 tablespoon clear honey
approx. 2 tablespoons milk

1. Sieve the flour and salt into a bowl and rub in the margarine till the mixture resembles fine breadcrumbs.
2. Stir in the sugar and walnuts, add the egg, honey and enough milk to form a soft dough.
3. Roll out on a floured surface to a thickness of 1½ to 2 cm / ½ to ¾ in. Cut into 5cm / 2in rounds with a plain cutter.
4. Put the scones on a greased baking sheet, brush the tops with milk and bake in the oven at 220°C / 425°F or gas mark 7 for 15 minutes until well-risen and golden-brown. Cool on a wire rack.

Drinks

Honey grapefruit shake (for one)

150ml / ¼ pint chilled milk
150ml / ¼ pint grapefruit juice
½ tablespoon clear honey

1. Mix the milk, grapefruit juice and honey until thick and frothy, either with a whisk or in a blender.
2. Pour into a tall glass.

Banana and pear shake

2 bananas, peeled
425g / 15oz tin of pears in unsweetened juice
6 tablespoons vanilla ice cream
275ml / ½ pint skimmed milk
ground cinnamon to decorate

1. Place the bananas, pears and juice, ice cream and milk in a blender and blend till smooth.
2. Pour into 4 glasses, sprinkle with cinnamon and serve.

Strawberry milk shake (for one)

110g / 4oz strawberries, washed
275ml / ½ pint cold milk
2 teaspoons caster sugar
1 scoop vanilla ice cream

1. Place all the ingredients in a blender and liquidise at the fastest speed for 15 seconds.
2. Pour into a tall tumbler and serve immediately.

Crunchy peppermint milk shake
(for one)

25g / 1oz plain cooking chocolate
3 tablespoons chocolate ice cream
150ml / ¼ pint cold milk
¼ teaspoon peppermint essence

1. Put the chocolate in a blender and chop finely.
2. Add all the remaining ingredients and blend for a further 30 seconds until well mixed and frothy. Serve at once.

Iced chocolate (for two)

275ml / ½ pint milk
150ml / ¼ pint single cream
3 tablespoons chocolate syrup
8 ice cubes

1. Whisk together the milk, cream and syrup.
2. Put the ice cubes in a jug, pour the chocolate mixture over them and serve.

Pine-lime sparkler

6 tablespoons lime cordial
275ml / ¹/₂ pint pineapple juice
8 ice cubes
575ml / 1 pint soda water
4 slices of lime

1. Divide the lime cordial and pineapple juice between 4 tall glasses.
2. Add 2 ice cubes to each glass and top up with soda water.
3. Decorate each glass with a slice of lime.

Morning refresher

2 bananas
2 tablespoons clear honey
2 eggs
1 litre / 2 pints unsweetened orange juice

1. Peel the bananas and put them into a blender with the honey and eggs. Blend and gradually add the orange juice.
2. Serve at once, with a slice of wholemeal toast.

Vivian's summer cooler

225g / 8oz fresh fruit: raspberries, strawberries, etc.
275ml / ¹/₂ pint natural yoghurt
575ml / 1 pint chilled milk
2 teaspoons honey

1. Put all the ingredients into a liquidiser and blend until smooth.
2. Serve in 4 tall glasses.

Juicy pick-me-up

275ml / ¹/₂ pint orange juice
150ml / ¹/₄ pint carrot juice
275ml / ¹/₂ pint apple juice
¹/₄ cucumber
6 ice cubes
sprigs of mint to serve

1. Put all the ingredients apart from the mint into a blender.
Blend until smooth.
2. Pour into a jug or glasses and decorate with the sprigs of
mint.

Caribbean drink (for one)

225ml / 8fl.oz milk
1¹/₂ tablespoons drinking chocolate
pinch ground nutmeg
pinch ground allspice
pinch ground cinnamon
1 tablespoon whipped cream
1 marshmallow

1. Bring the milk, chocolate and spices to the boil in a pan.
2. Remove from the heat, whisk thoroughly and pour into a
beaker.
3. Top with the whipped cream and marshmallow and
sprinkle on a little extra drinking chocolate.

Gemma's drink (for one)

150ml / ¹/₄ pint fresh orange juice
150ml / ¹/₄ pint natural yoghurt
1 slice of orange

1. Whisk or blend the orange juice and yoghurt.
2. Pour into a glass and add a slice of orange.

Peter Rabbit's drink (for one)

150ml / ¼ pint carrot juice
5 tablespoons milk
1 teaspoon honey

1. Put all the ingredients into a liquidiser or whisk thoroughly.
2. Pour into a tall glass and serve with a straw.

Recipes for festive occasions

ST. VALENTINE'S DAY

Valentine hearts

Cooking time: 10-12 minutes

225g / 8oz self-raising
   flour
1/2 teaspoon salt
150g / 5oz white
   vegetable fat, or half
   fat half margarine
approx. 275ml / 1/2 pint
   cold water
275ml / 1/2 pint whipping
   cream
strawberry jam
icing sugar for dusting

1. Sieve the flour and salt into a bowl. Cut the fat into small pieces and stir into the flour with a knife. Mix to a stiff paste with the cold water.

2. Roll the dough out on a lightly floured surface to a rectangle three times as long as it is wide. Fold the bottom third up, the top third down, and seal the edges by pressing with the rolling pin. Turn the dough half round so that one of the sealed edges is towards you and repeat the rolling out, folding and sealing. Turn half round again and do this once more. Always roll away from you.

3. Cover the pastry dough and leave in a cool place for 15 minutes.

4. Roll out the pastry on a lightly floured surface to $\frac{1}{2}$cm / $\frac{1}{4}$in thick, make sure that you roll away from you and do not press too hard.

5. Cut out heart shapes and place the hearts on a baking tray. Bake in the oven at 230°C / 450°F or gas mark 8 for 10-12 minutes, when they should be well risen and golden-brown.

6. Cool the hearts on a wire tray, then cut each through horizontally and sandwich back together with whipped cream and strawberry jam.

7. Sieve a little icing sugar on the top of each heart.

These should be eaten the same day while they are crisp.

Valentine dream

110g / 4oz plain chocolate
grated rind and juice of 1 orange
3 eggs, separated
150ml / $\frac{1}{4}$ pint double cream

1. Break the chocolate into pieces, put in a saucepan, add the orange juice and rind and melt gently. Leave to cool for 2-3 minutes, then stir in the egg yolks.

2. Whisk the egg whites until stiff.

3. Fold the egg white into the chocolate mixture. Spoon into 4 glasses or ramekin dishes and leave to cool for about 1 hour.
4. Whisk the cream until stiff and put on top to decorate.

PANCAKE DAY

Pancakes

Makes: 10-12

110g / 4oz plain flour
pinch of salt
275ml / ½ pint milk
50g / 2oz white vegetable fat

1. Mix the flour and salt in a basin, make a well in the middle and drop in the egg.
2. Stir with a wooden spoon, then gradually add milk, stirring all the time, until all the flour is worked in. Beat well and add the remaining milk.
3. Melt a small piece of fat in a frying pan. Pour in 2 tablespoons of batter, tilting the pan so that it covers the bottom.
4. When the pancake is dry on top and golden-brown underneath, turn it over and quickly cook the other side.
5. Put the pancake on a hot dish and use up the rest of the batter in the same way. Serve immediately with sugar or syrup, lemon or orange, or use one of the fillings on the next page.

Fruity pancake filling

2 tablespoons soft brown sugar
2 bananas, peeled and sliced
2 tablespoons fresh lemon juice
275ml / $\frac{1}{2}$ pint double cream
375g / 13oz tin of pineapple rings, cut into small pieces
25g / 1oz chopped nuts

1. Whip the cream until it forms soft peaks.
2. Lightly fold in the rest of the ingredients.
3. Spoon some filling on each pancake, roll them up and serve.

Cheese and apple pancake filling

225g / 8oz cream cheese
4oz raisins
1 medium-sized dessert apple, peeled, cored and chopped
grated rind of 1 lemon
caster sugar to serve

1. Mix the cream cheese, raisins, apple and lemon rind very thoroughly.
2. Spoon some filling on each pancake, roll them up, dust with caster sugar and serve.

MOTHER'S DAY

Simnel cake

Cooking time: 2½-3 hours

175g / 6oz margarine
175g / 6oz light brown sugar
3 eggs, beaten
225g / 8oz self-raising flour
pinch of salt
2 teaspoons mixed spice
175g / 6oz seedless raisins
175g / 6oz sultanas
110g / 4oz currants
75g / 3oz mixed peel
2 tablespoons milk
675g / 1½lb almond paste
honey
angelica

1. Cream the margarine with the sugar until light and fluffy. Gradually beat in the eggs, adding a little flour at the same time.
2. Sieve the flour with the mixed spice and salt, add the raisins, sultanas, currants and peel.
3. Fold into the first mixture, add the milk to give a soft dropping consistency. Leave in a cool place for 10 minutes.
4. Divide the almond paste into three equal portions. Roll out one third into a 18cm / 7in circle.
5. Place half the cake mixture in a greased and lined 18cm / 7in round cake tin and smooth the top.
6. Cover with the circle of almond paste and put the rest of the cake mixture on top. Make the surface level.

7. Bake in the centre of the oven at 150°C / 300°F or gas mark 2 for 2$\frac{1}{2}$-3 hours. If the cake starts browning too much, cover the top with some foil. Remove from the oven and cool in the tin.

8. Roll another third of the almond paste out to an 18cm / 7in circle. Take the cold cake out of the tin, brush the top with honey and cover with the almond paste circle.

9. Roll the remaining almond paste into 12 small balls. Cut 24 angelica leaves and arrange with the almond balls on top of the cake to decorate.

Gooey chocolate surprise

2 tablespoons apricot and pear spread
4 tablespoons chocolate or chocolate and hazelnut spread
1 tablespoon hot water
30 digestive biscuits, crushed
8 glacé cherries, chopped
50g / 2oz sultanas
1 chocolate flake, crushed

1. Mix the spreads with a tablespoon of hot water to soften.

2. Stir in the cherries, sultanas and crushed biscuits, and mix very well.

3. Press into a greased square tin and sprinkle the top with the chocolate flake.

4. Leave to chill in the fridge for 1 hour before cutting into squares.

Mother's day treat

Cooking time: 15 minutes

Makes: 10-12

75g / 3oz butter
75g / 3oz caster sugar
1 egg
150g / 5oz flour
$\frac{1}{2}$ teaspoon baking powder
few drops pure vanilla essence
milk to mix

buttercream:
40g / 1$\frac{1}{2}$oz butter
50g / 2oz icing sugar
few drops pure vanilla essence

1. Cream the butter with the sugar in a bowl. Beat in the egg, fold in the flour, then the vanilla essence and a little milk to give a soft dropping consistency.

2. Grease patty tins and half-fill with the mixture. Bake in the oven for about 15 minutes at 200°C / 400°F or gas mark 6. Remove from the tins and leave on a wire rack to cool.

3. In the meantime make the buttercream. Cream the butter till light, gradually beat in the icing sugar, then a few drops of vanilla essence, till the mixture is smooth and creamy.

4. Cut a thin slice off the top of the cup cakes and spread some buttercream on each. Cut the slices in half and stick in the buttercream to look like butterfly wings. Dust with a little icing sugar.

EASTER

Easter biscuits

Cooking time: 12-15 minutes

225g / 8oz self-raising flour
110g / 4oz caster sugar
110g / 4oz margarine
1 egg, beaten
grated rind and juice of ½ lemon
2 tablespoons currants

1. Mix the flour and sugar, rub in the fat with your fingertips.

2. Add the currants and the lemon juice and rind, and sufficient egg to make a stiff dough.

3. Roll out thinly and cut into rounds.

4. Place on a greased baking sheet and bake in the oven at 180°C / 350°F or gas mark 4 for about 12-15 minutes. Transfer to a wire rack to cool.

Easter fingers

Cooking time: 20 minutes

50g / 2oz milk or plain chocolate
5 tablespoons vegetable oil
175g / 6oz sugar
2 eggs
1 teaspoon pure vanilla essence
110g / 4oz self-raising flour
$^1/_4$ teaspoon salt
melted chocolate to cover

1. Melt the chocolate in a saucepan with the oil. Stir in the sugar, the unbeaten eggs and the vanilla essence.
2. Sieve the flour and salt together and add to the melted chocolate. Mix well.
3. Put the mixture in a greased tin and leave to cool in the fridge for 1 hour, then bake in the oven for 20 minutes at 200°C / 400°F or gas mark 6.
4. Leave in the tin to cool, then slice into fingers and cover with melted chocolate.

Hot cross buns

Cooking time: 20-25 minutes

Makes: 12

450g / 1lb white flour
50g / 2oz margarine
1 tablespoon dried yeast
pinch of salt

50g / 2oz caster sugar
2 tablespoons mixed spice
110g / 4oz currants
50g / 2oz mixed peel
150ml / ¼ pint lukewarm milk
75ml / 3fl.oz water
1 egg, lightly beaten

glazing:
40g / 1½oz caster sugar
4 tablespoons milk

crosses:
2 tablespoons strong white flour
2 tablespoons cold water

1. Sieve the flour and salt into a bowl and rub in the margarine. Stir in the dried yeast, caster sugar, spice, currants and mixed chopped peel.
2. Make a well in the middle and pour in the lukewarm milk, water and beaten egg. Mix well and then turn out the mixture onto a very lightly floured surface.
3. Now knead the dough, pushing it away from you and then back again so that you seem to be rolling it. Keep on kneading the dough for about 10 minutes until it has become smooth and elastic.
4. Oil two baking trays. Cut the dough into 12 even-sized pieces and knead each of them into a smooth ball. Put them, with plenty of space in between, on the baking trays.
5. Cover the buns with a damp cloth (this will prevent the dough from drying out) and leave them in a warm place to rise until they become twice the size, about 1 hour.
6. Glaze the uncooked buns by thoroughly mixing 2 teaspoons of the caster sugar and 2 tablespoons of the milk, and brushing the tops of the buns with this mixture.

7. To make the crosses, mix the flour with 2 tablespoons cold water to make a smooth paste. Spoon this into a small piping bag with a plain nozzle and then pipe a cross onto each bun.
8. Bake the buns in the oven at 200°C / 400°F or gas mark 6 until they are a dark golden-brown, about 20 minutes.
9. Meanwhile make more glazing, by heating the rest of the sugar and milk gently until dissolved, then boiling for 5 minutes.
10. Transfer the buns to a wire rack and brush at once with the milk and sugar syrup.

FATHER'S DAY

Irresistibles

Cooking time: 12-15 minutes

Makes: 12-14

75g / 3oz margarine
110g / 4oz brown sugar
110g / 4oz walnuts, chopped
50g / 2oz flaked almonds
50g / 2oz dried fruit, chopped
1 tablespoon wholemeal flour

1. Melt the margarine and sugar in a saucepan over a gentle heat.
2. Off the heat add all other ingredients and stir well.
3. Line a baking tray with parchment paper and put spoonfuls of the mixture well apart on the baking tray. Press into neat shapes.

4. Bake in the oven at 180°C / 350°F or gas mark 4 for 12-15 minutes, until golden.

5. Let the biscuits go cold on the tray before removing them from the parchment paper.

Spiced cake

Cooking time: 30 minutes

50g / 2oz margarine
110g / 4oz caster sugar
75g / 3oz dates, stoned and chopped
1 tablespoon coarse-cut marmalade
110g / 4oz self-raising flour
1/2 teaspoon cinnamon
1 egg
4-6 tablespoons milk
1 teaspoon caster sugar and 1/2 teaspoon cinnamon for topping

1. Sieve the flour and cinnamon into a bowl, and rub in the margarine.

2. Stir in the sugar, dates and marmalade and add the egg and milk to make a soft dough.

3. Put the mixture into a greased 18cm / 7in cake tin and sprinkle on the mixed cinnamon and caster sugar.

4. Bake in the oven at 180°C / 350°F or gas mark 4.

HALLOWE'EN

Pumpkin pie

Cooking time: 35-40 minutes

225g / 8oz self-raising flour
50g / 2oz margarine
30g / 2oz white vegetable fat
pinch of salt
2 tablespoons cold water

filling:
450g / 1lb pumpkin, peeled and de-seeded
1 tablespoon molasses
110g / 4oz soft brown sugar
2 eggs
25g / 1oz margarine
1 teaspoon cinnamon
grated rind of 1 lemon
50g / 2oz walnuts or pecan nuts to decorate

1. Sieve the flour and salt into a bowl, rub in the fat until the mixture resembles fine breadcrumbs.
2. Sprinkle the cold water over this mixture and stir in with the blade of a knife until a stiff dough is formed. If necessary knead lightly.
3. Roll the pastry out and line a 20cm / 8in pie tin.
4. Cut the pumpkin into medium-sized cubes and boil in water for about 20 minutes, until soft.
5. Mash the pumpkin, add all the other ingredients except the nuts and fill the pie case. Decorate with nuts.
6. Bake in the oven at 190°C / 375°F or gas mark 5 for 35-40 minutes. Allow to cool for 5 minutes before serving.

BONFIRE NIGHT

Baked potatoes

Cooking time: 1 hour

4 large potatoes
butter
salt and pepper

1. Scrub the potatoes clean.
2. Prick them all over with a fork and bake in a pre-heated oven at 200°C / 400°F or gas mark 6 for about 1 hour, depending on size. Test to see if they are cooked by pushing in a fork.
3. Cut a cross in the top of the potatoes and serve with butter and salt and pepper.

Stuffed baked potatoes

To make stuffed baked potatoes, bake the potatoes as in the preceding recipe. Then cut off a 'lid' from the top of each one. Scoop out some of the cooked potato, mix this with the filling, and put back into the shell. Re-heat in the oven for about 10 minutes.

Try the fillings below, or invent your own!

Quantities are for 1 potato.

2 tablespoons baked beans
50g / 2oz grated cheese
25g / 1oz cream cheese and a little finely chopped onion
2 tablespoons coleslaw
50g / 2oz peanut butter
50g / 2oz cream cheese and chopped pineapple

Guy Fawkes night treat

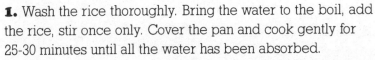

1 onion, chopped
2 tablespoons oil
110g / 4oz brown rice
700ml / 1¼ pint water
2 tablespoons wholemeal breadcrumbs
50g / 2oz Cheddar cheese, grated
1 tablespoon self-raising flour
1 egg
½ tablespoon tomato purée
sea salt to taste
freshly ground black pepper to taste

1. Wash the rice thoroughly. Bring the water to the boil, add the rice, stir once only. Cover the pan and cook gently for 25-30 minutes until all the water has been absorbed.
2. Gently fry the onion in the oil till soft. Mix with the rice and all other ingredients to make a thick mixture.
3. Shape into sausages – you can use an icing bag without the nozzle for this.
4. Brush the sausages with vegetable oil and grill on the barbecue rack, turning until both sides become golden-brown.
5. Serve with wholemeal finger rolls and relish to taste.

Guy Fawkes pie

Cooking time: 20 minutes

1 kilo / 2lbs potatoes
110g / 4oz margarine
2-3 tablespoons milk
2 onions, peeled and chopped
1 leek,chopped

4-6 vegetable burgers, diced
2 tablespoons soy sauce
450ml / 16fl.oz vegetable stock
salt
freshly ground pepper

1. Peel and boil the potatoes, mash them, adding 2oz margarine, the milk and salt and freshly ground pepper to taste.
2. Melt the rest of the margarine in a frying pan and add the onion and leek, cook for 2 minutes while stirring.
3. Now add the diced burgers, vegetable stock and soy sauce. Leave to simmer for 10-12 minutes.
4. Pour this mixture into an ovenproof dish and top with the creamed potato.
5. Brown in the oven for 20 minutes at 200°C / 400°F or gas mark 6.

CHRISTMAS

Christmas delight (for six)

This delicious dessert makes a change from Christmas pudding. It is served cold, and should be made the day before you want to serve it.

275ml / 10fl.oz natural yoghurt
275ml / 10fl.oz double cream
6 tablespoons soft dark brown sugar
flaked almonds to decorate

1. Whip the double cream in a medium-sized bowl, pour the yoghurt into the whipped cream and stir in gently.

2. Spoon the creamed mixture into 6 ramekin dishes or small glass bowls. Then sprinkle a tablespoon of sugar over the top of each.

3. Leave in the fridge overnight, remove about an hour before you serve the dessert and sprinkle with some flaked almonds.

Christmas Eve dream

Cooking time: 6-8 minutes

1 egg yolk
275ml / ¹/₂ pint single cream
2 teaspoons caster sugar
grated rind of ¹/₂ lemon
8 slices French bread, 2¹/₂cm / 1in thick
2 eggs
25g / 1oz margarine
2 tablespoons oil
caster sugar to dust
orange or lemon quarters to serve

1. Mix the egg yolk with the cream, sugar and lemon rind in a shallow dish.

2. Put the bread in this mixture and leave to soak for about 5 minutes.

3. Beat the eggs and dip the soaked bread slices in the egg.

4. Heat the margarine and oil in a frying pan until sizzling, then dry the bread slices until golden on the underside. Turn them over with a spatula and cook for a further 1-2 minutes.

5. Remove from the pan, drain on crumpled kitchen paper and dust with a little caster sugar. Serve with orange or lemon wedges.

Fudge and walnut cream

275ml / ½ pint whipping cream
275ml / ½ pint natural yoghurt
4 heaped tablespoons soft brown sugar
50g / 2oz walnuts, roughly chopped

1. Whip the cream until it is thick.
2. Using a metal spoon, fold in the yoghurt. Make sure you do
this thoroughly.
3. Spoon the mixture into 4 wine glasses and sprinkle a
heaped tablespoon of brown sugar onto each one.
4. Leave them overnight in the fridge. Next day the sugar will
have melted and formed a fudgy layer on the top.
5. Sprinkle with chopped nuts and serve.

Christmas cake

Cooking time: 4 hours

350g / 12oz self-raising flour
110g / 4oz ground almonds
1 heaped teaspoon mixed
   spice
225g / 8oz margarine
225g / 8oz soft brown sugar
4 large eggs
8 tablespoons milk or half
   milk and half brandy
225g / 8oz sultanas
225g / 8oz currants
225g / 8oz raisins
110g / 4oz glacé cherries, cut
   into quarters

110g / 4oz candied peel, chopped
almond paste (see next page)
royal icing (see next page)

1. Sieve the flour and mixed spice, add the ground almonds.

2. Cream the margarine with the sugar in a large bowl.

3. Beat the eggs with the milk and brandy. Stir the flour mixture and eggs alternately into the creamed margarine, just a little at a time.

4. Add all the fruit and mix well.

5. Grease and line a 22cm / 9in round or 20cm / 8in square cake tin. Put the cake mixture into the tin and smooth the top with a knife. Bake in the oven at 150°C / 300°F or gas mark 2 for about 4 hours. Check regularly after the first hour to make sure that the cake does not brown too much on top. If necessary put some foil over the tin.

6. When it is cooked turn the cake out onto a wire rack to cool. Then wrap in greaseproof paper and put in an airtight tin till you are ready to ice the cake just before Christmas. The cake will taste better for being stored for a while.

7. No less than 2 days before Christmas apply the almond paste. Cut the top of the cake level if you want. Measure round the sides with a piece of string. Divide the almond paste into two equal portions, then halve one of the portions again and form into 2 rolls. On a surface dusted with icing sugar roll each out into a strip as wide as the height of the cake and half as long as the piece of string. Now brush the sides of the cake with honey or sieved apricot jam and press the strips of almond paste on. Smooth the joins with the blade of a knife. Roll out the remaining almond paste to fit the top of the cake. Brush the top with honey or jam and cover with the almond paste. Press down firmly and trim the edges if necessary. Leave for at least 24 hours to harden.

8. Put the almond-pasted cake on a board and spoon half the icing on the top. Use a palette knife dipped in cold water to spread the icing evenly over the top of the cake. Then cover the sides of the cake with icing, again using a palette knife to spread and smooth it.

9. You can now decorate the top of the cake if you wish, for instance by adding some green colouring to a piece of left-over almond paste and cutting it into small holly leaf shapes and colouring another piece red to make berries.

Almond paste

Covers a 22cm / 9in round or 20cm / 8in square cake

350g / 12oz ground almonds
175g / 6oz caster sugar
175g / 6oz icing sugar
1 large egg, beaten
juice of ½ a lemon

1. Sieve the icing sugar into a bowl. Add the ground almonds and caster sugar. Mix together.

2. Add the lemon juice, then the beaten egg to make a pliable paste.

Royal icing

Covers a 22cm / 9in round or 20cm / 8in square cake

900g / 2lbs icing sugar
5 egg whites
2 teaspoons lemon juice for hard icing or 2 teaspoons
   glycerine for a softer icing

1. Lightly beat the egg whites with the lemon juice or glycerine.
2. Sieve the icing sugar and add half to the egg whites. Beat very well.
3. Add the remaining icing sugar. Stir very well until stiff and smooth.

Christmas stuffing

Cooking time: 35-40 minutes

175g / 6oz fresh wholemeal breadcrumbs
juice of ¹/₂ a lemon
50g / 2oz margarine
1 medium-sized onion, peeled and finely chopped
1 egg, beaten
25g / 1oz dried apple, chopped
50g / 2oz dried prunes, finely chopped
2 teaspoons mint, fresh or dried
pinch of salt and pepper

1. Melt the margarine in a large frying pan and cook the onion until tender but without letting it go brown.
2. Add the chopped fruit and the breadcrumbs, and fry, stirring all the time, for about 4-6 minutes.
3. Remove the frying pan from the heat, pour in the lemon juice and add the chopped mint. Then stir well with a wooden spoon.
4. Add pepper and salt to taste and the beaten egg and mix everything together thoroughly.
5. Shape the mixture into 12 balls.
6. Place the stuffing balls on an oiled baking tray and cook in the oven at 190°C / 375°F or gas mark 5 for 35-40 minutes until a lovely golden-brown.

Serve hot.

Mince pies

Cooking time: 15-20 minutes

Makes: 20

225g / 8oz self-raising flour
50g / 2oz margarine
50g / 2oz white vegetable fat
pinch of salt
25g / 1oz caster sugar
2 tablespoons cold water
350g / 12oz vegetarian mincemeat
1 egg, beaten

1. Sieve the flour and salt into a bowl and rub in the fats with your fingertips till the mixture resembles fine breadcrumbs. Stir in the sugar. Sprinkle the cold water over the mixture and stir in with the blade of a knife till a stiff dough is formed. If necessary knead lightly.
2. Place the pastry on a floured surface and roll out very thinly. Cut out 20 8cm / 3in rounds and 20 5cm / 2in rounds.
3. Line 20 tartlet tins with the larger pastry circles, half fill with mincemeat. Brush the edges of each pastry lid with water, and press on top to seal the edges. Pierce a hole in the centre of each lid with a knife to allow steam to escape.
4. Brush the top of each mince pie with beaten egg and bake in the oven for 15-20 minutes at 230°C / 450°F or gas mark 8.
5. When cooked leave in the tins for a few minutes, then take them out and place on a wire rack to cool.
6. When they are cold you can dust them with sieved icing sugar. Keep in an airtight container.

Snow fool (for two or four)

2 egg whites
1 tablespoon lemon juice
2 tablespoons caster sugar
275ml / ½ pint apple purée or other puréed fruit
glacé cherries
fresh cream or grated nuts
sponge fingers to serve

1. Put the egg whites into a bowl and whisk until stiff,
gradually whisk in the lemon juice, sugar and fruit purée.
2. Spoon into 2 glass dishes or 4 ramekins, top with a little
fresh cream or grated nuts, and cherries. Serve snow fool with
sponge fingers, as soon as possible after making it.

Chocolate cherry truffles

Makes: 32

175g / 6oz dark chocolate
50g / 2oz margarine
350gl / 12oz plain cake crumbs
110g / 4oz icing sugar, sieved
2-3 tablespoons orange juice
110g / 4oz maraschino cherries, chopped
chocolate vermicelli, icing sugar or flaked chocolate pieces

1. Break the chocolate into small pieces and put in a saucepan with the margarine. Heat gently on the stove till melted.
2. Take off the heat and stir in the cake crumbs, icing sugar, orange juice and cherries. Leave in the fridge until firm enough to handle.
3. Form spoonfuls into small balls. Roll in vermicelli, icing sugar or flaked chocolate.
4. Put in paper cases. Chill in the fridge to set.

NEW YEAR'S EVE

New Year welcome

Filo pastry is available ready-made from most supermarkets or from a delicatessen. It will keep for up to two months in the freezer.

Cooking time: 23-25 minutes

12 sheets filo pastry
vegetable oil or melted butter
1 teaspoon ground cinnamon
50g / 2oz sultanas
grated rind of 1 lemon
6 apples
1 tablespoon icing sugar for dusting

1. Defrost the filo pastry, then keep it covered with a damp cloth. Take the sheets one by one and brush them lightly all over with oil or melted butter.

2. Line a 22cm / 9in shallow, loose-bottomed flan tin with 10 sheets of filo pastry, leaving the pastry hanging over the sides. Cover with a cloth so that it does not go dry while you prepare the filling.

3. Peel and core the apples and cut into 1cm / $^{1}/_{4}$in pieces. Mix with the sultanas, cinnamon and lemon peel. Spoon the mixture into the filo-lined tin.

4. Carefully lift up the pastry which is hanging over the sides and gently fold it over the filling. Press it down lightly.

5. Cut the last 2 sheets of filo pastry into 2$^{1}/_{2}$cm / 1in wide strips and arrange them twisted or curled up on top to decorate.

6. Bake in the oven at 180°C / 350°F or gas mark 4 for 18-20 minutes. Remove from the oven and with oven gloves carefully remove the tin. Place the pastry on a baking tray and return to the oven for another 5 minutes to give the sides a crispy texture.

7. Place on a wire rack for a few seconds while you dust it with icing sugar. Serve hot with custard, yoghurt or cream or just on its own.

Also published by Green Print

The Green Cook's Encyclopedia
JANET HUNT

If you want to know practically everything there is to know about
cruelty-free food and vegetarian cooking, this alphabetical handbook
gives you instant information on every ingredient you can think of.
There are detailed cooking hints, hundreds of recipes, historical
information, and advice on buying and storage.

Plus instant guidance on such diverse subjects as barbecues, baby
food, veganism, dieting and macrobiotics.

Experienced cooks will find a mine of useful information here, while
newcomers to the kitchen table will welcome a book that answers all
their questions . . .

ISBN 1 85425 057 4

£7.99

In stock at all good bookshops, or by post (add 60p postage) from
Green Print, 10 Malden Road, London NW5 3HR.